JAMES MacNAUGHTON
Est 1864

GUNMAKERS

21 Frederick Street Edinburgh EH2 2NE

CN00656131

DAVID McKA...

GUNMA...

32, HAMILTON ROAD, BOTHWELL, GLASGOW G71 8NA

D. H. SINNERTON
Master Gunmaker

APPRENTICE TO JAMES PURDEY & SONS

LONDON

Gun & Rifle Maker

OAKWOOD · GROUSE ROAD · ENGLAND

Westley Richards & Co.
fine guns & rifles since 1812

GUN & RIFLE MAKERS

Inventors & Patentees of
Breech Loading Guns & Rifles, Cartridges & Bullets

130 Pritchett Street
Birmingham, England

BY APPOINTMENT TO
HRH THE DUKE OF EDINBURGH
RIFLE MAKERS

BY APPOINTMENT TO
HRH THE PRINCE OF WALES
SUPPLIERS OF BESPOKE GUNS, SHOOTING
ACCESSORIES & COUNTRY CLOTHING

HOLLAND & HOLLAND
Established 1835

BRUTON STREET, LONDON WI

P. V. NELSON
Gunmaker

MAKERS OF BEST SHOTGUNS & DOUBLE RIFLES

LONDON

T. R. WHITE & CO
(GUNMAKERS)

Oakedge Park
Staffordshire England

WILLIAM & SON

GUN & RIFLE MAKERS
14 MOUNT STREET LONDON WI

BY APPOINTMENT TO
H·I·M THE SULTAN OF TURKEY
THE SHAH OF PERSIA.

GOLD MEDAL.
LONDON 1904

GOLD MEDAL.
LONDON 1904

PRIZE MEDALS.

1864

1882

PRIZE MEDALS.

WATSON BROS.
GUN & RIFLE MANUFACTURERS

39 REDCROSS WAY,
LONDON BRIDGE · SE1

REMOVED FROM 29 OLD BOND ST., FORMERLY DURS EGG, ESTABLISHED IN THE REIGN OF KING GEORGE III

To Colin
with all my love
(Enjoy !
p x
Christmas 2010

The
Best of British

A CELEBRATION OF
BRITISH GUNMAKING

The Best of British

A CELEBRATION OF
BRITISH GUNMAKING

DAVID GRANT AND VIC VENTERS

Quiller

Copyright © 2010 David Grant (photographs)
Copyright © 2010 Vic Venters (text)

First published in the UK in 2010
by Quiller, an imprint of Quiller Publishing Ltd

British Library Cataloguing-in-Publication Data
A catalogue record for this book
is available from the British Library

ISBN 978 1 84689 069 7

The right of David Grant and Vic Venters to be identified as the authors of this work has been asserted in accordance with the Copyright, Design and Patent Act 1988

The information in this book is true and complete to the best of our knowledge. All recommendations are made without any guarantee on the part of the Publisher, who also disclaims any liability incurred in connection with the use of this data or specific details.

All rights reserved. No part of this book may be reproduced or transmitted in any form or by any means, electronic or mechanical including photocopying, recording or by any information storage and retrieval system, without permission from the Publisher in writing.

Book and Jacket Design by Sharyn Troughton
Printed in China

Quiller

An imprint of Quiller Publishing Ltd
Wykey House, Wykey, Shrewsbury, SY4 1JA
Tel: 01939 261616 Fax: 01939 261606
E-mail: info@quillerbooks.com
Website: www.countrybooksdirect.com

Contents

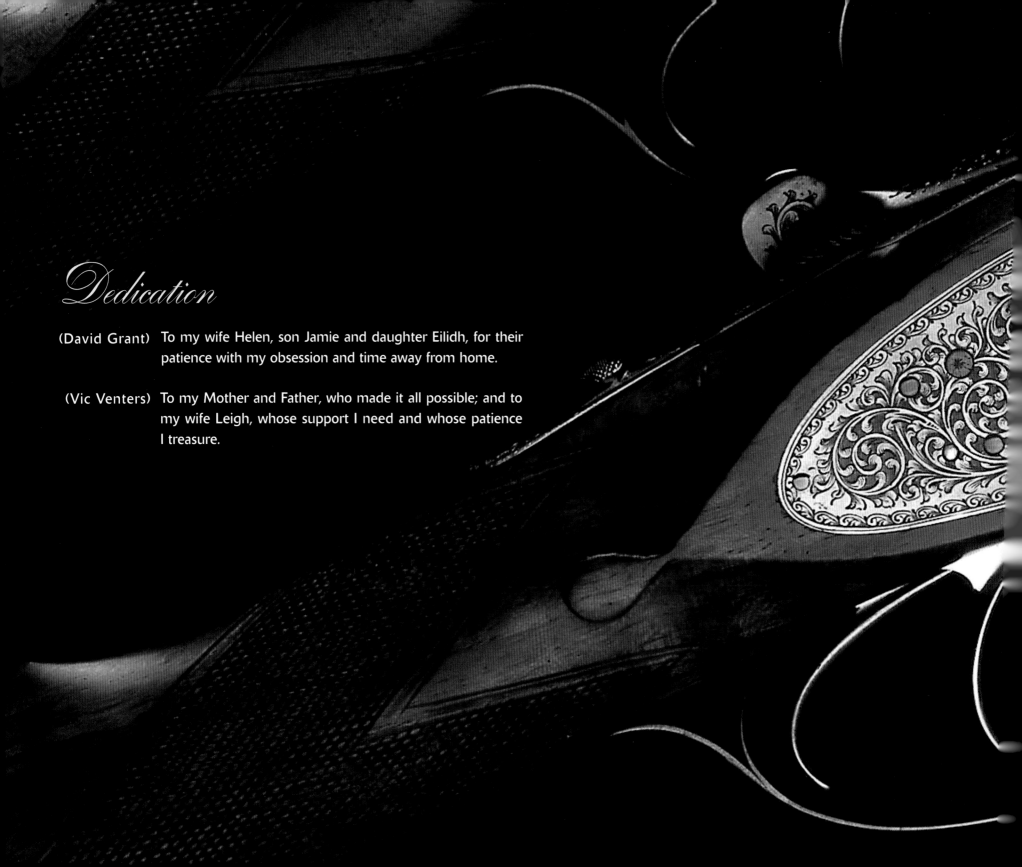

Dedication

(David Grant)   To my wife Helen, son Jamie and daughter Eilidh, for their patience with my obsession and time away from home.

(Vic Venters)   To my Mother and Father, who made it all possible; and to my wife Leigh, whose support I need and whose patience I treasure.

Acknowledgements

Even a modest book like this depends on the friendships and assistance of many. We are indebted to the following for helping create the images and text for this book:

Without the craftsmen of Britain – alive or deceased, working in the UK or abroad – this book would never have been possible. Many gunmakers have willingly cooperated and shared their time and expertise when we interfered with their production. In the end this is their book, not ours.

David Grant thanks Mark Cumpston for his companionship. He also thanks Nick Phillips, Philippa and Phil for their skill in scanning transparencies and eliminating blemishes, and all those at Quiller Publishing for their skills and for many months of hard work.

Vic Venters thanks the editors he has worked with over the last two decades, especially: Chuck Wechsler, of *Sporting Classics*; Daniel Cote, of *The Double Gun Journal*; Silvio Calabi, former publisher of *Shooting Sportsman*; John Ian Gregson, former editor of *The Shooting Times & Country Magazine*; Jonathan Young, of *The Field*; Mike Barnes, of *Fieldsports*; and Will Hetherington, of the *Shooting Gazette*. Two colleagues have been especially important: Jim Dean and Ralph Stuart, both my friends and the latter my editor (and comrade in the trenches of publishing) at *Shooting Sportsman*. Likewise Douglas Tate, author of *Birmingham Gunmakers* and *British Gun Engraving*, provided much advice and informed perspectives on British gunmaking. John Ian Gregson, fellow woodcock shooter, has been a wonderful host on my many visits to the UK. Michael McIntosh has long provided inspiration and sound advice.

For those in the British Gun Trade, or those associated with it, a special thanks: Ian Andrews of James Purdey & Sons; William Asprey of William & Son; Ted Atkinson of T.R. White & Co.; G.O. Baker of Thomas Bland & Sons; Toby Barclay of Heritage Guns; Chris Batha of Charles Boswell; Nigel Beaumont of James Purdey & Sons; Bill Blacker, barrelmaker; Peter Blaine of James Purdey & Sons; Alan Bower of Atkin Grant & Lang Ltd; Alan and Paul Brown, engravers; Robin Brown and his father, the late Sidney Brown of A.A. Brown & Sons; Alexe and David McKay Brown of David McKay Brown (Gunmakers) Ltd; Ian Clarke of James Purdey & Sons; Simon Clode of Westley Richards & Co.; Phil Coggan, engraver; Mike Cooley and Alan Crewe of Cogswell & Harrison (Gunmakers) Ltd; Malcolm Cruxton of G.M. Cruxton; Steve Denny of Holland & Holland Ltd; Ken Duglan of Atkin Grant & Lang Ltd; Stephane Dupille, gunstock maker; David J. Dryhurst of W.W. Greener Ltd; Paul Faraway of Holland & Holland Ltd; Alfred Gallifant, gunmaker; Gavin Gardiner of Gavin Gardiner Ltd; Daryl Greatrex of Holland & Holland Ltd; Graham Greener of W.W. Greener Ltd; Ken Halbert of Westley Richards & Co.; Graham Halsey of Boss & Co.; Roger Hancox, Proof Master, The Birmingham Gun Barrel Proof House; Andrew Harvison of Holloway & Naughton; Gary Hibbert, actioner; Ron Holden, gun-trade patron; Nicholas Holt of Holt's Auctioneers; Ken Hunt, engraver; Charles Lee, engraver; Robert M. Lee, gun-trade patron; Roger Lees, ex-Proof Master, of The Birmingham Gun Barrel Proof House; Hugh Lomas of H.G. Lomas Gunmakers, Inc.; Michael Louca of Watson Bros Gunmakers; Scott Luard formerly of William & Son; The late Don Masters (and his widow Valerie) of E.J. Churchill; Peter V. Nelson of P.V. Nelson (Gunmakers); Bruce Owen, gunmaker; Leslie A. Paul, gunmaker; Alastair Phillips of William Evans Ltd; Peter and David Powell of William Powell & Sons; Richard Purdey of James Purdey & Sons; Jack Rowe, gunmaker; Carl Russell of Atkin Grant & Lang Ltd; The late Harold Scandrett of A.A. Brown & Sons; Steve T. Sidki, gunstock blank supplier; David Sinnerton of D.H. Sinnerton Gun & Rifle Maker; Mike Smart, stock finisher; Mary Smith of C.H. Smith & Sons; Peter Spode, engraver; Mark Sullivan, gunmaker; Dale Tate, gunmaker; David Trevallion of Trevallion Gunstocks; Richard Tandy of W.W. Greener Ltd; Robert Turner of Turner Richards Gunmakers; Anthony 'Trigger' Alborough-Tregear of Westley Richards & Co.; Frank, John and Brian Wiseman of F.J. Wiseman & Co. Ltd; Paul West of William & Son; Tony White of T.R. White & Co.; Roland Wild of Holland & Holland Ltd; Russell Wilkin of Holland & Holland Ltd; Reginald York and Robert Wallin of York & Wallin Ltd.

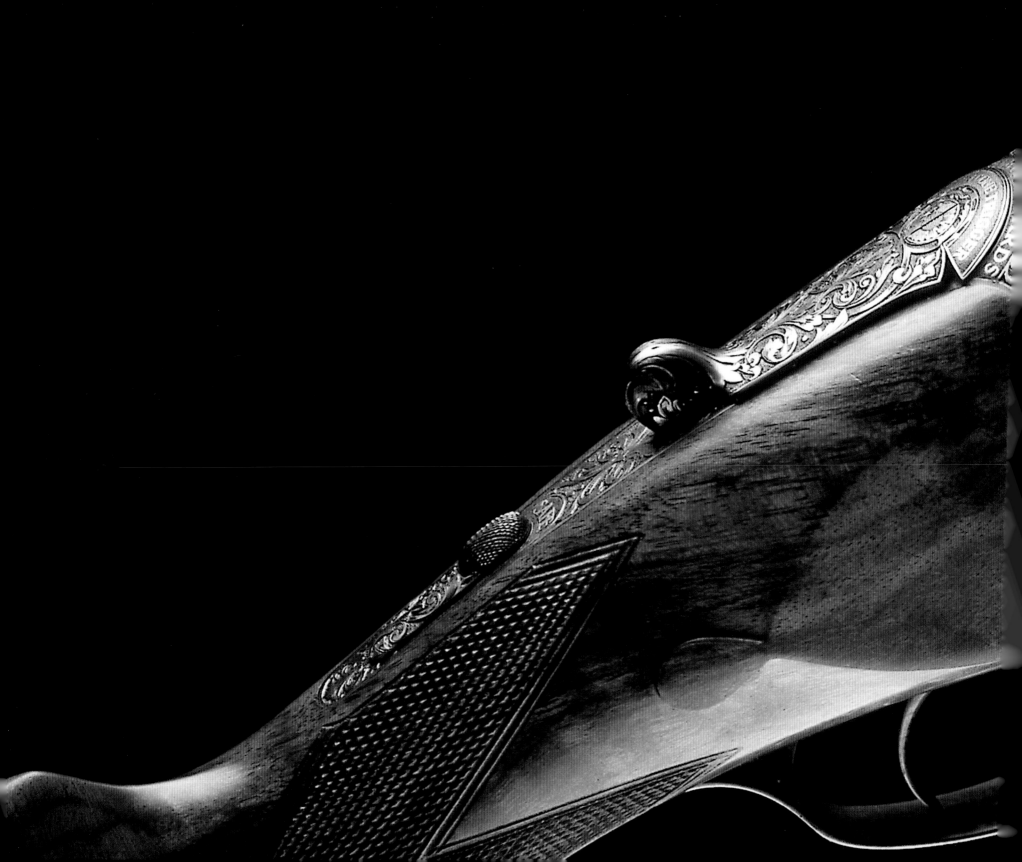

WESTLEY RICHARDS

Preface

American journalist *Walter Lippmann* once wrote that the press 'is like the beam of a searchlight that moves restlessly about, bringing one episode and then another out of darkness into vision'.

In many respects Lippmann's comment is relevant to the book you hold in your hands. *The Best of British* is a tribute to the great guns and gunmaking craftsmen of Britain, casting a light on them through the lenses of David Grant's superb photography.

Our focus is on guns made in the last thirty or so years, although there are historical examples scattered throughout the book – in the latter case either noteworthy or unusual guns, or images that are particularly arresting, or sometimes a combination of both.

I emphasise guns made in the last thirty years because of the renaissance in both the quality of sporting guns produced in Britain, and revival of the gunmakers themselves. As a professional photographer for the last four decades – and as one of the most sought-after photographers to the British gun trade for the last three decades – David Grant has witnessed and recorded this renaissance with his work for the majority of Britain's gunmakers.

Many makers have been (and continue to be) his clients for advertising, catalogue, or archival work, while he has photographed the guns of others for editorial publication in leading British and American sporting and fine-gun magazines. His work as photographer for *British Gun Engraving* (Safari Press, 2000) gained him unparalleled access to the world's greatest collections of modern sporting guns, which reside in the United States.

Walter Lippmann went on to qualify his searchlight comment by noting that the episodic nature typical of media coverage was not truly sufficient to reveal complete understanding of issues – and in this sense *The Best of British* is not a full history of contemporary sporting arms production in the UK. In fact, David Grant initially conceived of it as a modest, self-published tribute to the best guns he had photographed in recent years. When demand for Grant's twenty-image booklet quickly outstripped supply, friends and professional colleagues suggested he might have latched on to something with larger potential. We are happy to report Andrew Johnston at Quiller Publishing agreed.

The result is this work, with captions providing specific information on the guns pictured and their makers, as well as supplementary text that supplies basic historical information, addresses and facts, as well as context on current production (where applicable). As cultural objects every firearm has a story to tell – particularly bespoke guns made to order by individual craftsmen – and where possible we have contacted makers for details.

That said, *The Best of British* is not intended to be a technical treatise in the tradition of W.W. Greener, Major Sir Gerald Burrard or Gough Thomas, nor does it furrow new historical ground, as have recent works by Donald Dallas, Don Masters, Graham Greener, Douglas Tate or Nigel Brown.

What we hope it provides is an introduction to some of the individual craftsmen responsible for making today's best British sporting arms – an emphasis that was overlooked historically or deliberately suppressed by writers in the more socially stratified milieu of the late nineteenth and early twentieth centuries.

'Our curiosity', writes British psychotherapist Adam Phillips 'depends on a receding horizon'. In this case the receding horizon is the kind of traditional craftsmanship practised by your grandfather's gunmaker. Most (though not all) of the guns featured in this book were made by craftsmen who were bench-trained before the advent – or at least the gun trade's adoption of – computer-assisted design and manufacture. Many of these craftsmen are nearing retirement, or are in the last decade of their careers. As David's photographs illustrate, their skills are as polished as any from much-heralded halcyon periods in the past.

This does not mean we are in the last golden age of best British gunmaking – but there is a convincing argument to be made that we are in the last golden age of traditional craftsmanship. Increasingly sophisticated technology means that best British guns will be made well into the future, but they will not necessarily be made by men whose trade, in Gough Thomas's words, is 'traceably descended from that of the medieval armourer'.

Media coverage of gunmakers, particularly in modern times, has mostly been centred on the London-makers. Exceptions tend to be those makers that advertise, as editorial copy (on both side of the Atlantic) tends to chase marketing money, and smaller craftsmen who either cannot afford to advertise, or whose skills make it redundant, simply haven't received public accolades they deserve. In very modest measure we hope this book helps rectify this.

Lastly many of Britain's recent 'High Art' guns have tended to vanish into the collections of those who commissioned them, and if resold they pass hands privately, rather than go to auction, where they might otherwise be viewed by the larger public or photographed for wider dissemination. This work is no complete catalogue of such, but we hope it offers a glimpse at guns rarely seen.

But enough of words already – enjoy the tour of some of Britain's very best guns.

Vic Venters

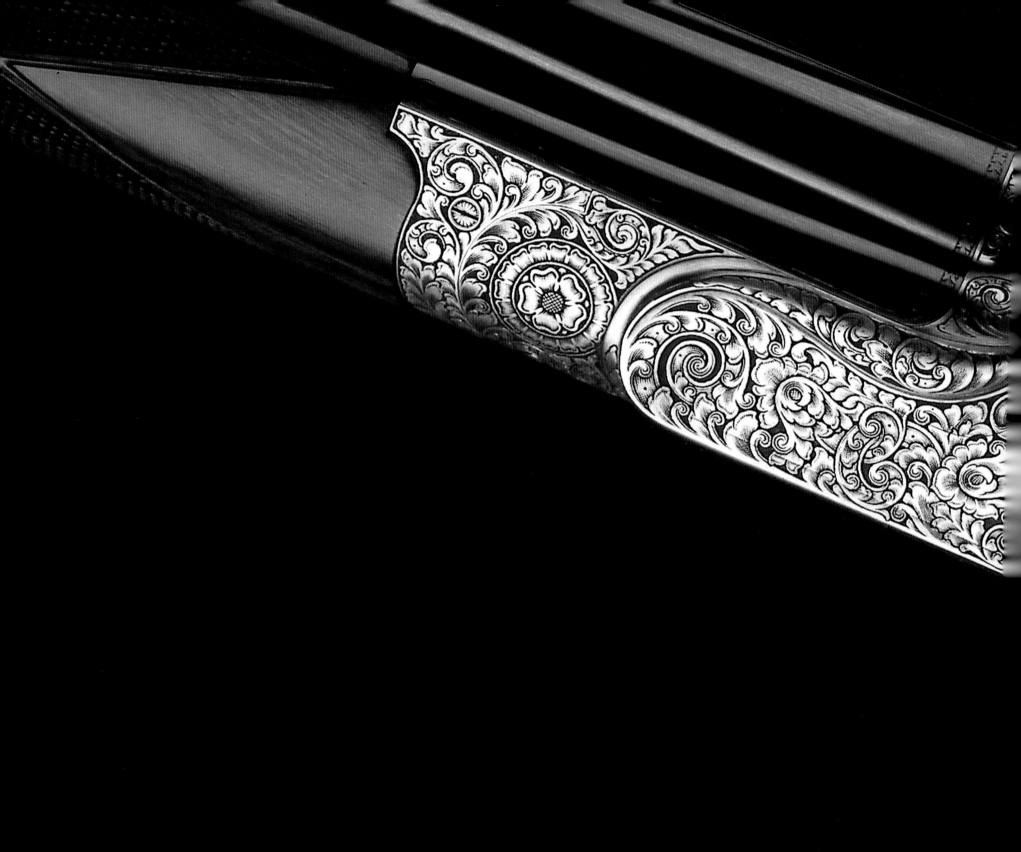

Introduction

Turns in the tide of history are not always easy to fathom but December 1980 marked a winter in which the British gun trade plumbed the bottom of its fortunes.

Churchill, Atkin Grant & Lang Ltd – along with a bevy of makers under its umbrella – stopped trading. The firm, which consolidated some two centuries of storied London gunmaking and included Watson Brothers, Frederick Beesley, Charles Hellis, and Charles Lancaster, had crashed into a wall raised by towering inflation and a stricken economy.

'It was a sad time,' recalled W.W. Greener gunmaker Richard Tandy, who had trained as an actioner at Churchill in the 1970s. 'Throughout the trade there was a feeling the whole thing could disappear.'

But ten years later Britain's gunmakers had not disappeared; instead each of the names from the 1980s' debacle was trading again in one form or another, or soon would be. Holland & Holland was purchased in 1989 by Chanel Ltd, which infused capital needed to modernise and remarket, a move mirrored five years later when France's Vendome purchased Purdey. Best-quality boutique makers with craftsmen at the helm were by then emerging – in London, for example, Peter V. Nelson was catching the eyes of international collectors and in Glasgow David McKay Brown was solidifying his reputation as Scotland's pre-eminent gunmaker. Even in Birmingham, long languishing in repair work, Westley Richards, among others, was beginning to stir.

From its Dunkirk in the late seventies to today, the British gun trade has recovered in surprising ways – if not in the quantity of guns once produced then in their quality and variety. Great designs have been revived: Boss-type over/unders, Scotland's Round Action, Westley's hand-detachable 'droplock', W.W. Greener's G-grade gun, Purdey's hammergun, to name some of the more notable. Moreover, after almost a century's slumber, mechanical innovation awakened in Britain in the 1990s with McKay Brown's Round Action over/under, Holland's 'Royal' sidelock over/under, Watson Brother's rounded-body over/under, as well as with Anglicised productions of Italian-inspired detachable-triggerplate designs, notably by Holland & Holland and, of late, by Purdey.

British engraving is today again among the most vibrant in the world. No longer are the best English engravers masters only of traditional scroll, but now also of bulino, exuberant carving and chasing, as well as inlaying multi-coloured gold and other precious metals.

David Grant's images in *The Best of British* capture proof of this revival. Some of the new guns pictured are familiar in customary form and decoration; the design and embellishment of others – though exotic by traditional standards – is now part of, I would argue, the mainstream of contemporary British gunmaking and decoration. Which begs the question: how did we get here from there?

'Art follows empire,' Sir Joshua Reynolds once observed, and since the end of the Second World War, so too have buyers of British guns. In the latter half of the twentieth century, Americans have dominated the market, especially with London's largest makers like James Purdey and Holland & Holland.

'The Second World War left Europe bankrupt,' said auctioneer Gavin Gardiner, who has managed Sotheby's sporting gun department and also worked at Boss & Co. 'Britain was still paying for all those lend-lease Tommy guns and Sherman tanks over five decades later, with rationing continuing into the fifties and a Labour government introducing taxes and death duties that bankrupted English society. There were virtually no new gun orders coming from the home market.'

Instead it was the dollar that acted like oil in the machine in the post-war period. 'For a period of forty years, from 1960 to 2000, Americans probably accounted in some years for up to seventy-five per cent of our new gun orders,' said Richard Purdey, retired chairman for the firm that bears his family's name. 'American customers have been extremely important to Purdey's, and to all the other surviving London gunmakers, since the end of the war.'

If Americans helped keep the motor running in the last half of the century – certainly for the top crust of London's trade – it is worth briefly examining how this patronage has also transformed the British gun itself. A Texas oil baron and an English lord might share the same language (in a manner of speaking) but the gulf spanning respective values could be as wide as the Atlantic. With Americans as primary benefactors, it was inevitable that their cultural preferences would eventually become manifest in British guns.

Up through the early 1950s, aristocratic ideals broadly dominated design and decoration, especially of best-quality guns. First and foremost they were tools made to kill game birds efficiently, and when built to best standards they invariably exuded a certain quiet grace and understated refinement. 'Decoration was subtle,' said Gardiner. 'It would be vulgar to have an overly ornate or flashy gun, so most were restricted to discreet rose and scroll under a delicate colour-hardened finish. Best-quality timber was used for stocks, but again nothing overly fancy as strength was a priority over beauty.'

Notwithstanding the occasional show gun (notably W.W. Greener's 'St George' and the like), or special commissions by Indian princes, British gun decoration, in the main, had been inherently conservative since the early nineteenth century. J.N. George, in *English Guns and Rifles*, observed: 'By degrees the English sportsman … came to view all unnecessary forms of embellishment with suspicion, as affording a means by which a slovenly maker might seek to distract attention from his own shortcomings in other and more important respects.'

Post-war Americans, economically and politically ascendant, often had other ideas. In 1961, gunwriter Gough Thomas quoted an English newspaper article: ' *"When I open my guncase, I want everyone to gasp," an American recently instructed Purdey's the gunsmiths…The paragraph was accompanied by a photograph of a lock-plate on which bob-white quail were inlaid in different shades of gold, à la Faberge.'*

Despite dramatic differences in decoration from the past, many of the guns from the 1950s and 1960s (often engraved by Ken Hunt) were still intended for shooting game and for use afield. Under glittering raiment, their fundamental function as an implement remained intact. This would begin to change, especially in the prosperous 1980s as the trade's revival gained momentum.

'A big change occurred in the mid-eighties when a new generation of collectors and enthusiasts entered the market,' said Gardiner. 'It is their influence that has dictated the trend in gunmaking over the last twenty-five years.'

This is exemplified by the 'High Art Gun' – a firearm built to the very finest standards with lavish embellishment to match, but never made with any intention of shooting, much less for rambles through briar and brush. Art guns are made as modern-day museum pieces from the beginning, commissioned with the intent of showcasing the finest craftsmanship possible in gunmaking, engraving, woodworking, and case making.

Some observers – and I admit I am one – believe today's Art gun has transformed the definition of what a best gun is, whether British-made or otherwise. 'There is no question that the relationship between guns as objects to use and as "Art Objects", or even "Investment Objects", has changed beyond recognition,' said Gardiner. 'In many cases these are definitely art first, and gun second, and up to about 1985 this was hardly ever the case. There is no doubt that today because of the enormous influence these clients have had that best guns are today viewed first as *objets d'art* – like an Italian sportscar or an expensive wristwatch.'

Richard Purdey, on the other hand, doubts the dichotomy between art and artefact of sport has altered the essence of a best gun – or necessarily its purpose: 'For the serious collector his specially commissioned engraving on a new bespoke Purdey is undoubtedly providing him with an *objet d'art,*' he said. 'For the wealthy businessman, who always wanted to make a fortune so that he could enjoy the best things in life, such as a fine house, a country estate, the grouse moor, a brace of Bentleys and Ferraris, and of course a new pair of Purdeys, I suspect that he still regards all these more as the best that money can buy, with aesthetic pleasure to be gained from looking at them as well as using them. Thus to him they are still more about form and function than art.'

Russell Wilkin, Holland & Holland's long-serving technical director of gunmaking, thinks the emphasis on Art guns may be overblown. 'I think the concentration on all the fancy stuff by the gun magazines and glossy coffee-table books gives a false impression,' he said. 'The vast majority of H&H guns and rifles are sold to active shooters with conservative tastes in embellishment.'

'In a nutshell,' concluded Richard Purdey, 'it is the customer – not us – who decides whether he is buying an *objet d'art* or a gun. We make guns.'

If there remains room for defining what a best British gun is – or has or has not become – there is no doubt that American demand for Art guns has raised the standards of British craftsmanship since the early 1980s. 'When the American collectors came on the scene it gave the gun trade a tremendous impetus,' said David McKay Brown. 'They insisted on upgraded wood, and much better engraving and finish. This was something different from what had come before.'

The influence on engraving, for example, is especially conspicuous. 'I cannot stress too much the effect American customers, especially the big collectors, have had on my work,' explained Phil Coggan, one of Britain's most talented engravers and whose work figures prominently in this book. 'I don't think I would be doing the same work without them. They have allowed me to produce very elaborate multi-coloured flush, raised, and carved gold work, as well as carved steel and very fine bulino.'

Although Art embellishment is engraving at its most rarified – and expensive – flashier aspects of its aesthetics have trickled down to 'standard' guns. Rather than quiet case colours produced by traditional pack hardening, silver-finish or 'bright' guns today prevail. Wood is today invariably well figured, sometimes sumptuous at the expense of strength. Although rose and scroll and traditional patterns remain ubiquitous, bulino game scenes, bold scroll, and complex ornamental work are far more common than three decades past, and better executed.

'The desire for more complex and elaborate engraving by US collectors did a huge amount to encourage and improve this particular art form,' said Richard Purdey. 'Gun engravers worldwide have Americans to thank for the enlargement of their numbers and providing a demand for their skills, and for demanding higher standards of work, and for taking such a passionate interest in their work – which in itself is great encouragement to do better.'

The latter-day emphasis on embellishment has also altered how modern sporting guns are priced, especially on the second-hand market. On guns made before, say, the 1960s, the maker's name and reputation (along with condition) were always sacrosanct in establishing value. This is no longer necessarily the case. 'Basically the engraver's name today drives the market value of modern "Art" guns,' says one American collector who is arguably the world's most prolific and influential patron of new best guns (and who prefers to remain anonymous). 'The maker's name remains important, but is no longer as important.'

Concordant with advances in engraving has come the restoration of best-quality craftsmanship in gunmaking. By the mid-1970s, a thirty-year shortfall in the trade's recruitment of craftsmen (and retention of them) had become evident in many British guns, particularly with lapses in engraving and finishing.

Today, the craftsmen who persevered through those difficult times, and who have subsequently burnished their skills meeting demands of persnickety collectors, are arguably among the finest to ever wield file and chisel in Britain. There are certainly fewer of them than ever before, and the consequent imbalance in supply and demand has had ramifications.

For one, the cost of commissioning a best gun today is truly gasp-inducing. Best guns have always been dear, but the disparity in prices between good-quality serviceable guns and best guns has never been greater. Compensating skilled labour in ever-short supply factors large in this equation. The upshot for craftsmen, however, has been economic empowerment. A skilled artisan commands good money nowadays, particularly those who have left a factory to work on their own.

'When I started at Purdey's in the seventies we could make a living,' explained David Sinnerton, a gunmaker and one of Britain's top outworkers to the trade. 'But it wasn't a great living.'

'By the time I left eleven years later', added Sinnerton, 'things had changed. Wages were better, and if you were good and went out on your own and worked hard you could make a very comfortable living.'

The shortage of craftsmen has also led to the more skilled and ambitious of them to be able to establish retail businesses – either under own names or buying an historic one – reversing consolidation dating to at least the late nineteenth century. 'The lack of a surplus supply of craftsmen allowed "real" makers to partly take the upper hand,' said A.A. Brown's Robin Brown, whose Birmingham firm made a successful transition in the mid-seventies from working anonymously for the trade to retail gunmaking. 'I would like to think we were at the forefront of this trend in the latter half of the century – craftsmen becoming "masters" rather than "men".'

Craftsmen-led firms that have been most successful have tended to be those that have found a niche to fill, or created one – Scotland's David McKay Brown with his Round Actions being a good example. This is not to suggest that best boutique makers have supplanted larger historical makers like Purdey, Boss, Holland & Holland and Westley Richards, only that buyers today enjoy a real diversity of guns, gun types, and gunmakers not seen in many decades.

This renaissance of traditional craftsmanship has occurred, ironically, against the backdrop of a technological revolution – the gun trade's widespread adoption of computer-assisted design and aerospace-inspired manufacturing – or as bench-trained craftsmen call it: 'The Machine'.

Introduced into best-gunmaking circles decades ago by Italy's Ivo Fabbri, CAD/CAM today influences almost all British makers, large or small. Without it, British production would be miniscule today, and guns even more expensive – perhaps utterly unaffordable. It unquestionably allows flexibility in manufacturing; design changes can be made quickly and efficiently, and it has facilitated the reintroduction of classic, difficult-to-build guns such as the Boss over/under or Westley's 'droplock'.

This leads us to examples pictured herein. While I have argued for transformative American effects, the guns remain emphatically British in character, and this is still their great attraction. At its core, British craftsmanship remains distinctive – from the sculpting and shaping of actions and fences to stock proportions to finishing to barrel blacking to colour-case-hardening. 'Almost every country is capable of producing machine-made goods,' noted Thomas Girtin, in *Nothing But The Best*, 'yet comparatively few have been able to rival the English craftsmen.'

The game gun – the best game gun – evolved in Britain, in its workshops and in its coverts, and while it has been successfully replicated elsewhere, and even improved mechanically, imitators often lack the subtleties of beauty that seems organic to the guns of Albion.

While the American influence has indeed been considerable, the home market has once again become important, notably in the last decade or so. There are, in fact, some very successful makers today with very few American customers. The Continent, likewise, is now a healthy market East to West, and may even supplant America one day as the primary market. In ten years, we may be speaking of the Russian influence on British gunmaking. Or in three decades, the Chinese…

And the future?

Events have ways of sinking prophecy and speculation, especially those steered by the capricious currents of global economics. One structural trend, however, seems certain to hold course: technology is increasingly skilful in imitating what once only human hands could perform, and there is nothing to suggest this trend will abate. Craftsmen from the pre-CNC era are also fast retiring, or nearing the age to do so, and those that replace them will be scarce and, perhaps, trained in techniques that are closer to fine-assembly work than old-fashioned gunmaking.

Does this mean the end of great British guns?

I think not, if we can go by the best work of the best Italian trade, which has increasingly gone the high-tech route. The foundering of the British trade has been predicted for at least a hundred years, and here it is, chugging into the twenty-first century, throwing a smaller wave off its bow nowadays, but one that still ripples through gunmaking worldwide.

The risk – if it lurks beneath the surface – is a subtle one. The ancient Greeks held that beauty resulted not from perfect symmetry but from that which was *almost* so. The possibility is that best British guns of the future made mostly with 'the machine' will be too perfect – devoid of the tiny mathematical imperfections in proportions that result from hand-work, imperfections that are almost invisible yet lend a hand-crafted gun its individuality and, for lack of a better word, its 'soul'.

Soul, however, is in no short supply in *The Best of British*.

Vic Venters

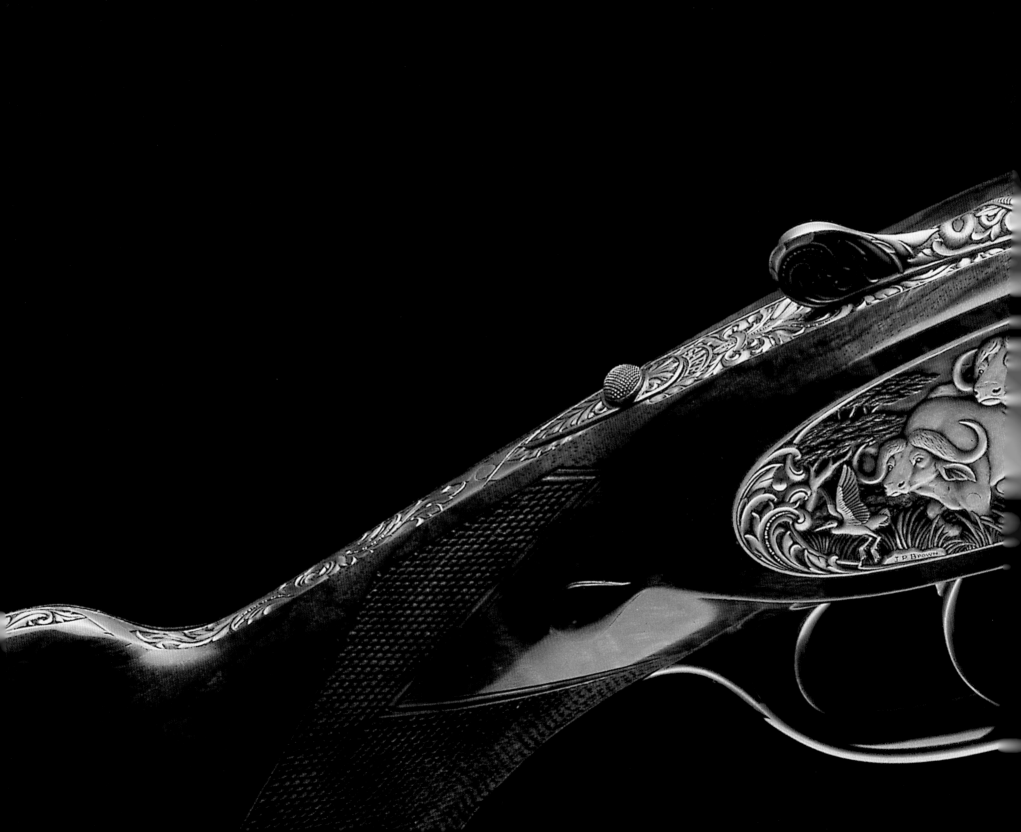

The Guns

PLATE 1

Henry Atkin 20-bore Sidelock

Henry Atkin No. 804 was ordered in 1903 by American banking magnate J.P. 'Jack' Morgan, Jr, as a gift for his son, Junius S. Morgan, then aged eleven. Smallbores were largely regarded as 'boys' or ladies' ' guns but unlike many 20-bores of the era – which tended to be mid-grade boxlocks – No. 804 was a fully engraved toplever bar-action sidelock ejector. Fitted with 29-inch barrels, it superficially appears to be a modern sidelock but it is actually a transitional late nineteenth century design made on a Perkes action (Patent 10679-86) and fitted with Deeley ejectors (Patent 14526-84). The action itself was purchased by Atkin in 1894 from Birmingham's W. & C. Scott & Sons, and was no doubt finished off by the former's craftsmen at the later date. The gun remained in Morgan-family hands until 2004, when it was stolen in a burglary. It was later recovered by a Morgan heir, then sold to Ken Duglan, who restored it in Atkin Grant & Lang's workshop.

PLATE 2

Thomas Boss 12-bore Tube-Lock

Though not of his invention – rather that of mentor Joseph Manton – Thomas Boss favoured the tube-lock. Though superseded by other percussion designs, Boss continued to build them into the 1850s. Tube-locks retained their favour with some shooters because of their ultra-reliable ignition, and any example by Boss will be built to best standards. Note that many of the signatures of the 'modern' British best are well developed on this circa 1840s Boss – sleek forend and a high-combed, straight-gripped stock devoid of ornamentation, trim lightweight barrels, and an elegant bowed trigger guard.

PLATE 3

Thomas Boss Exhibition Percussion Pistols

This pair of ornate percussion pistols are signed 'Thos Boss' and are believed to
have been built for the Great Exhibition of 1851. They are of superlative quality,
but are not typical of the restrained British aesthetic of that period, and instead
have many hallmarks of Continental styles – latticed, carved chequering; chiselled
and chased mounts; and elaborately carved butt caps. The damascus barrels are
actually lined with a steel inner-barrel. Thomas Boss only rarely made pistols, and
these are clearly two of a kind.

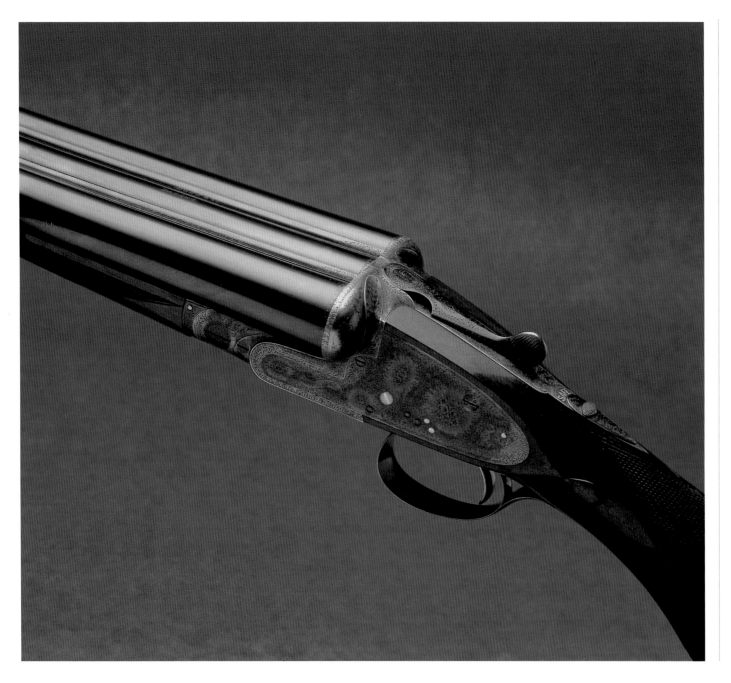

PLATE 4

Boss & Co. 16-bore Three-barrel Sidelock

Three barrels, one trigger, five pulls (two of them involuntary), three shots, 139 parts: such is the mechanical marvel of Boss sidelock No. 4690. It is the second of two three-barrel sidelocks ever built by Boss – the first being finished in 1898 as an exercise in gunmaking excellence, and also built as a way to promote the reliability of the then-new Boss single trigger. No. 4690, pictured here, was ordered shortly thereafter by Italian client Signore W. Baldo as a '16 bore Top snap 3 barrel gun. Patent single trigger, steel brls 28 in long. Press down forepart. Gold oval.' Finished in 1901, the gun has conventional sidelocks for barrels right and left, with the centre lock mounted on the triggerplate. The Boss trigger was modified to cope with two involuntary pulls, rather than one, during the firing sequence: right barrel, then centre, then left. Stephen Grant-style fluted fences help relieve any impression of ungainly width across the fences, and the gun is surprisingly light – only 6lb 14oz – and it handles with all the liveliness one would expect of a Boss.

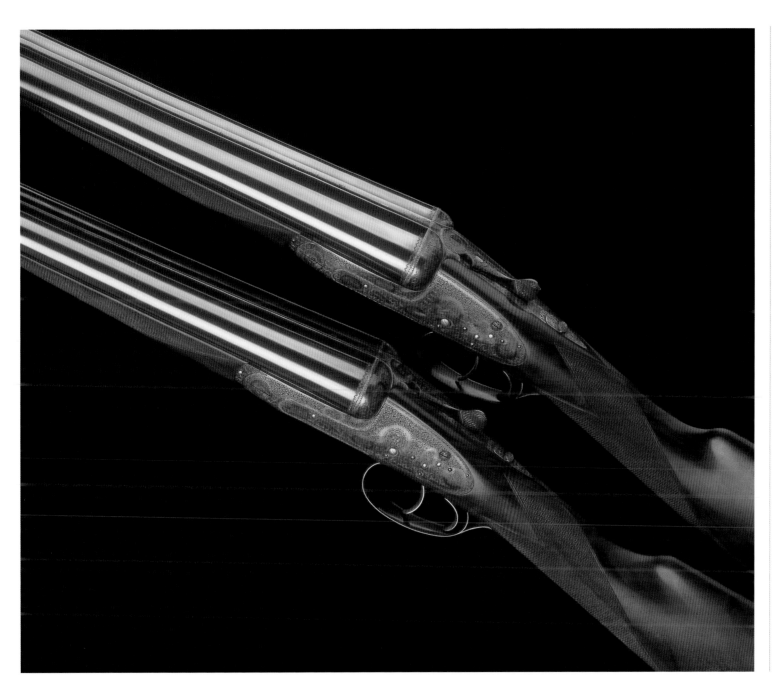

PLATE 5

Pair Boss & Co. Rounded-Body 12-bore Sidelocks

Boss & Co. proprietor John Robertson was not only a mechanical genius but an aesthetic innovator *nonpareil*. In the 1890s, Boss introduced the rounded-body sidelock: the action bar was shorn of beads, the width of the breech was reduced, the drop points and borders were dropped from the stock, and its wrist was made more cylindrical. Highly influential, the rounded-body design has since been widely copied in Britain and abroad, though few gunmakers have carried it off with anything like Robertson's original panache. This pair of 12-bores was engraved by Dave Tallett and completed in 2009.

PLATE 6

Pair Boss & Co. 12-bore Sidelocks

Although Boss is famous for its rounded-body sidelocks, historically the majority were made with conventional square actions. Even today, about fifty per cent of side-by-sides will be ordered with the latter action – such as this recently completed pair of 12-bores engraved by London's Andy Miles. His stylised bold scroll is atypical decoration for Boss guns, though in recent years non-traditional engraving patterns have become more common.

PLATE 7

Pair Boss & Co. 12-bore Sidelocks

Classic Boss: this pair of 12-bore sidelocks have traditional colour-case-hardened bar-action frames and double triggers, and were engraved by Dave Tallett with rose and scroll inspired by historic London engraver John (Jack) Sumner, whose tight-scroll patterns with multiple rose bouquets are virtually synonymous with Boss & Co. Dave Tallett, well known for his fine scroll, has created his own engraving dynasty, with talented sons Brad and Wesley following in his footsteps.

PLATE 8

Boss & Co. 12-bore Sidelock Over/Under

The Boss sidelock over/under, introduced in 1909, remains the world's most influential design of its type. John Robertson's novel use of bifurcated lumps and a barrel-bolting system eliminated the need for under-lumps, thereby reduced the height of the action, and helped produce a gun that was slim and lightweight yet fantastically strong. This recently completed pair of 12-bores was engraved by Christophe Rizzuto, originally trained in Liege, and now the first in-house Boss engraver in many decades.

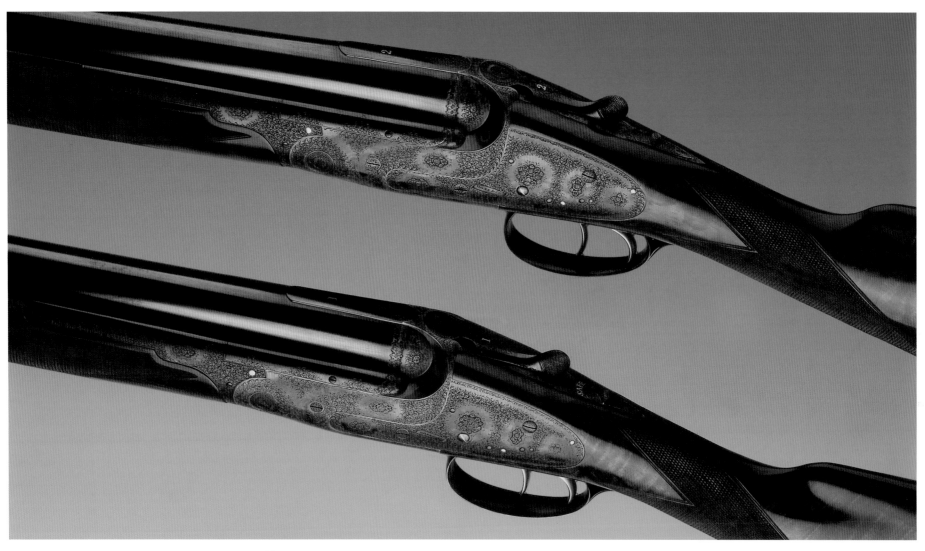

PLATE 9

Pair of Boss & Co. 12-bore Over/Unders

This pair of Boss 12-bore over/unders showcases the firm's round-bodied style, with no vestigial bead left on the action, and made without top ribs on the barrels. Over/unders currently comprise about sixty-five per cent of new orders, and Boss-style rose and scroll – like this by Dave Tallett – makes up about seventy per cent of engraving requests. Double triggers on over/unders, as seen here, are comparatively rare.

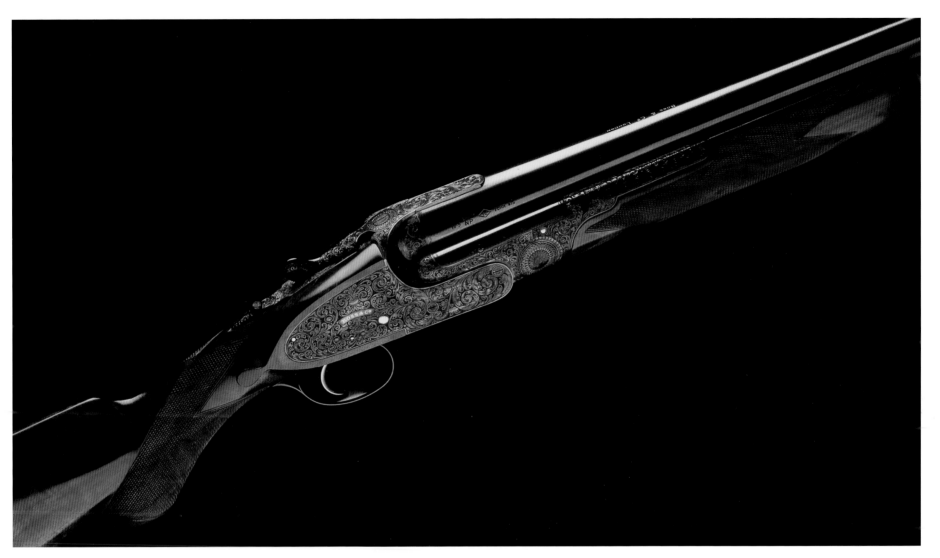

PLATE 10

Boss & Co. 12-bore Over/Under

This 12-bore over/under, engraved with bold scroll by Geoff Moore, has the traditional-shape action and is fitted with the Boss single trigger. Compared to its main London rivals, Boss has chosen a more conservative approach to the use of modern CNC machining, and much of the action filing – the carving and shaping of fences, for example – remains the purview of craftsmen with hammers, chisels and files. Boss's single trigger remains faithful to the 1894 design, and the company today has two in-house specialists trained to make it.

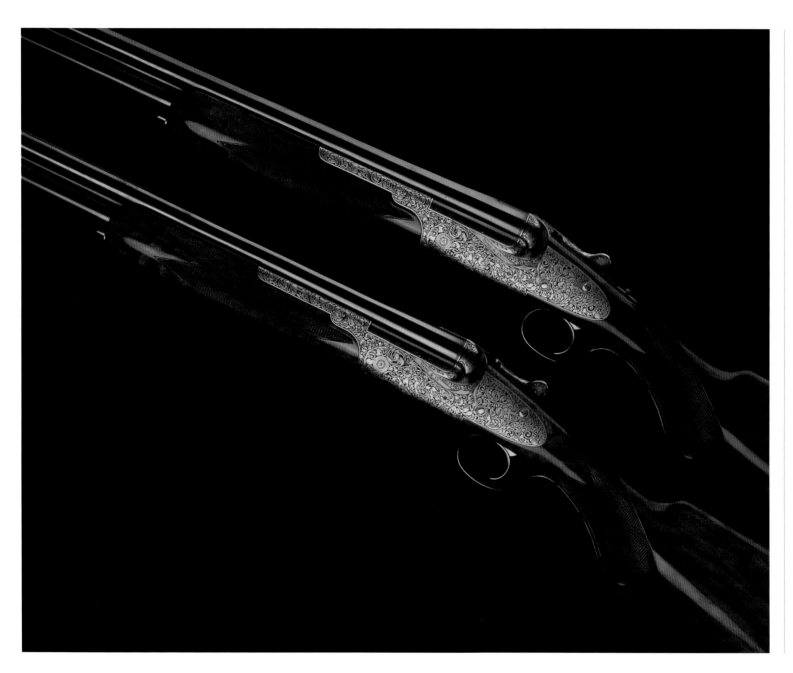

PLATE 11

Boss & Co Pair 20-bore Over/Unders

Andy Miles engraved this pair of 20-bore Boss over/unders. With 30-inch barrels they weigh only 6¼lb each – very lightweight for sidelock over/unders. These were made with rounded-body actions and also lack top ribs. Most Boss over/unders today are ordered without top ribs – not for weight issues, rather for aesthetics. 'Round-bodied Boss guns look amazing without the top rib's straight lines,' notes Managing Director Graham Halsey. Sans top-rib does save weight, however; the rib weighs about 3 to 3½oz, so when the gun is balanced by removing weight from the stock up to ½ pound can be shaved from each gun.

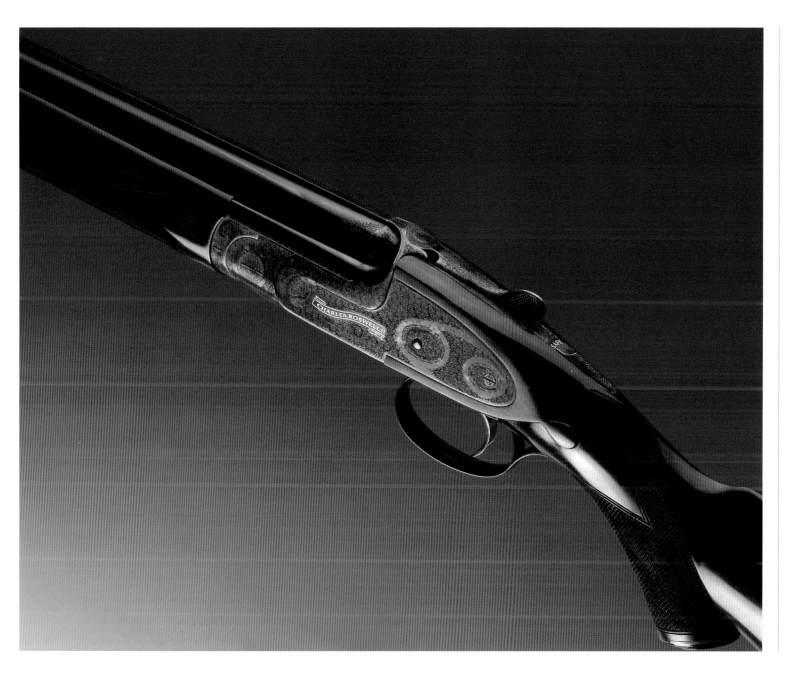

PLATE 12

Charles Boswell 28-bore Sidelock Over/Under

Completed in 2009 this Boswell 28-bore sidelock over/under was built on a current Churchill-style action under the direction of Boswell owner Chris Batha. Lee Butler, ex-Westley Richards and of Churchill, assisted with actioning, Scott Woods, ex-Purdey, struck and polished the barrels, and Bobby Smith, ex-Purdey, stocked the gun. It was engraved with rose and scroll in Italy at *Il Bulino Srl*, a cooperative of ten engravers working under Diego Bonsi.

PLATE 13

Charles Boswell .410 Sidelock Over/Under

A 'Baby Boswell' – a .410 sidelock over/under recently completed on a properly scaled Italian-sourced (FAMARS) action. Before finishing, the action was completely stripped and reshaped by Lee Butler and the barrels and ribs were profiled and polished by Scott Woods. It was stocked by Bobby Smith, engraved with fine rose and scroll by Dave Tallett, colour-hardened at Richard St Ledger's, and finished by Gerry Swanson. Smallbore sidelock Boswells have been popular in the United States, where they are favoured for quail and dove shooting.

PLATE 14

A.A. Brown & Sons 12-bore Sidelock

A.A. Brown No. 79587 was built in 1965 and is emblematic of the quality the firm was producing in-house during an era when many others in the British gun trade were slipping. Dating from the era when Brown was largely a maker to the trade, it is one of the first best-quality sidelocks to be commissioned by a private customer. The gun was engraved by Les Jones in standard Holland-style cutaway scroll, with scroll 'sunbursts' running up the barrels from the breeches. It has chopper-lump barrels, disc-set strikers, a fluted action with detachable locks made by Stanton & Co. Aside from the locks it was made entirely by Brown's in-house craftsmen: actioned by Albert H. Brown, jointed by Harry Homer, barrels machined and bored by Harold Scandrett, stocked by Albert Thompson and Robin Brown, colour-hardened by Ted Stokes, and finished by Sidney Brown. It remains in pristine condition, as photographed in 2009.

PLATE 15

A.H. Brown 12-bore Easy-Opening Boxlocks

A friend of Albert Henry Brown had him make this pair of easy-opening boxlocks in 1981 on the 'Connaught' pattern that Brown built for Westley Richards in the 1960s and early seventies. Connaughts have thicker sidewalls and slightly thinner recesses for lockwork than standard Anson & Deeleys, permitting them to be filed up rounder. Scott leverwork was used, as were rocker safeties, and this pair had Holland-type easy openers fitted. Albert Brown did all the actioning (note the Westley-style scroll-back action), while his A.A. Brown & Sons sourced the materials and otherwise made the gun. The pair was engraved by Walter Howe, at one time the chief engraver for Webley & Scott. In addition to these guns, Albert built another pair of boxlocks and a single sidelock under his own name.

PLATE 16

A.A. Brown Rounded Action 12-bore Supreme De Luxe Sidelock

Built in 1991, this A.A. Brown Supreme De Luxe is from the first pair to receive Robin Brown's semi-rounded action with its softened contours extending back through the stock. The action retains the double bar and flutes, and the stock keeps traditional drop points, but both were rounded at the client's request to give the gun the look and feel as if worn at the edges from long use. It proved popular with Brown's clients and has become the firm's signature style since. The gun was engraved by Keith Thomas with his lush interpretation of rose and scroll, with gamescene vignettes on the undersides of the actions.

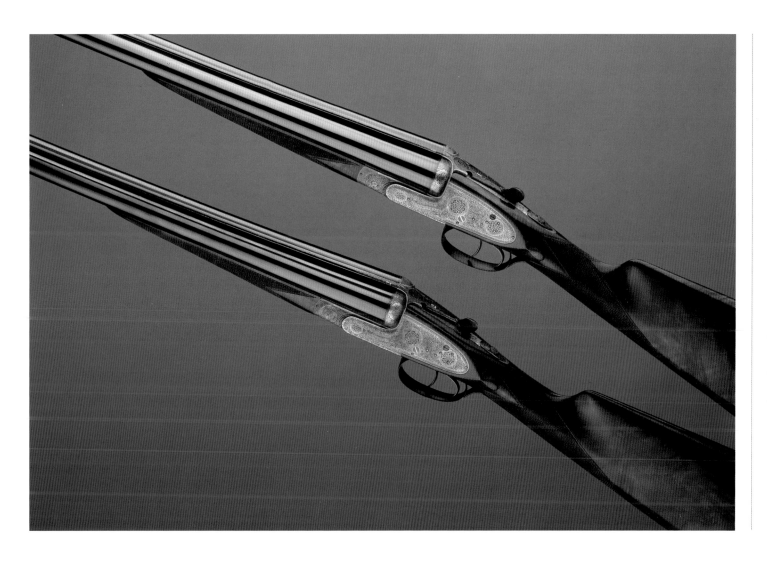

PLATE 17

Pair of A.A. Brown 12-bore Supreme De Luxe

The Supreme De Luxe has been A.A. Brown's standard bearer since the firm finished up orders for the trade in 1974 and began building guns under its own name for retail clients. Made on Brown's semi-rounded, easy-opening Holland-type action, this pair was engraved by Keith Thomas. Eschewing modern computer-assisted technology, Brown remains one of England's most traditional gunmakers.

PLATE 18

David McKay Brown 12-bore Round Action

Since McKay Brown's reintroduction of Scotland's Round Action in 1974, the shooting public has increasingly come to associate the design with the Glasgow maker. McKay Brown's version remains remarkably similar to the original Dickson design, although the former has made some subtle improvements – bolstering the forend iron, for example – and actions and components are today machined from modern alloy steels. This 12-bore weighs 6lb 10oz and is engraved with a traditional cutaway scroll pattern.

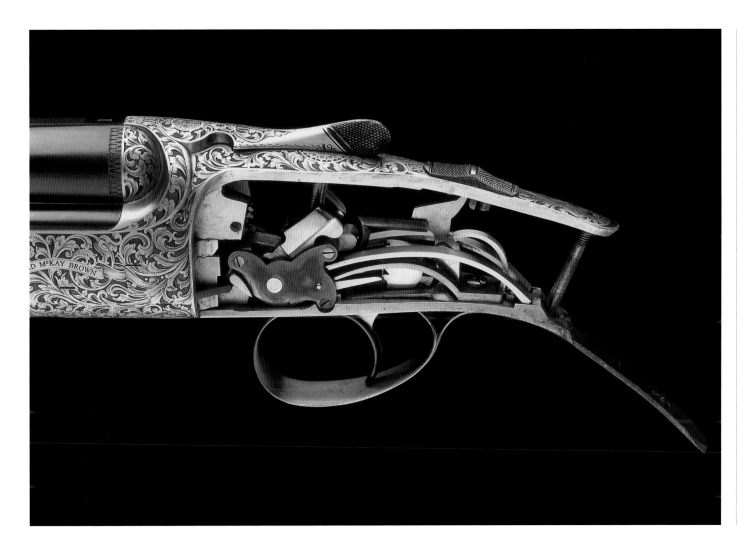

PLATE 19

David McKay Brown 12-bore Round Action Over/Under, stock removed

Sans stock, the triggerplate lockwork of this over/under reveals how its location to the rear of the action allows the latter to be rounded. McKay Brown's introduction of an over/under version in 1992 was not only Scotland's first new shotgun design in the twentieth century, but it has gone on to become a notable commercial success.

PLATE 20

Pair of 12-bore David McKay Brown Over/Unders

In recent years, McKay Brown's British customers have increasingly been seeking heavier, longer-barrelled over/unders suitable for high pheasant and sustained clay shooting. McKay Brown has adjusted his o/us to incorporate barrels up to 32 inches, longer forends, stocks with pistol grips and more ample proportions, wider ribs, chokes regulated for long ranges, single triggers and weights up to $8^1/_2$lb. These shown here, with 31-inch barrels and cutaway floral scroll, are David's personal pair for pheasant shooting, and weigh 7lb 10oz each.

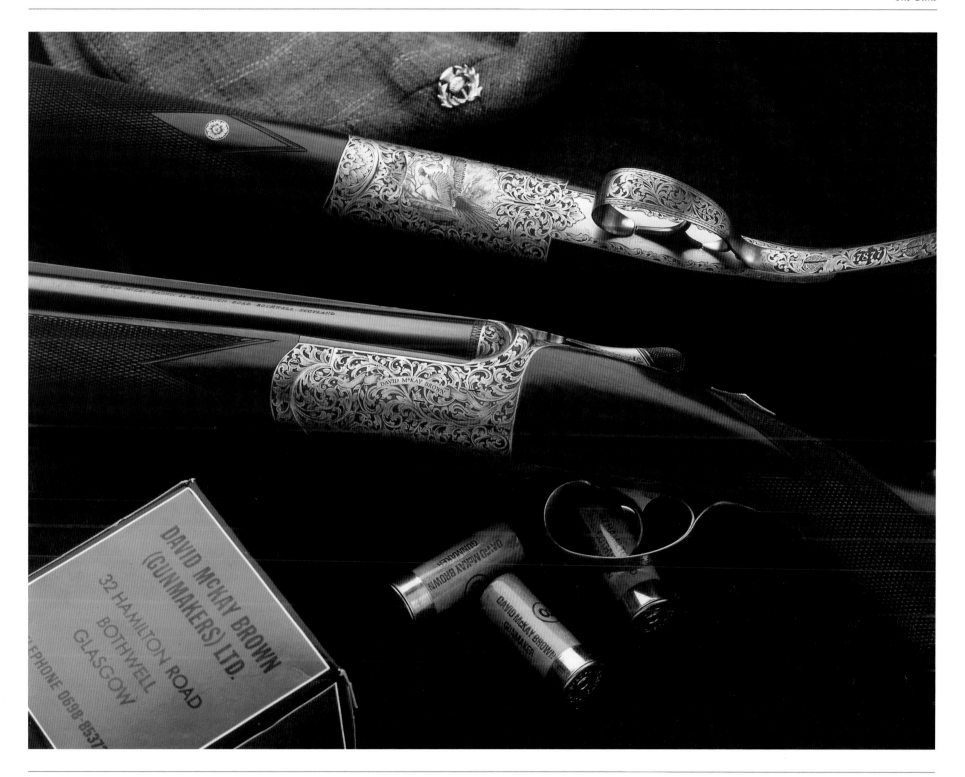

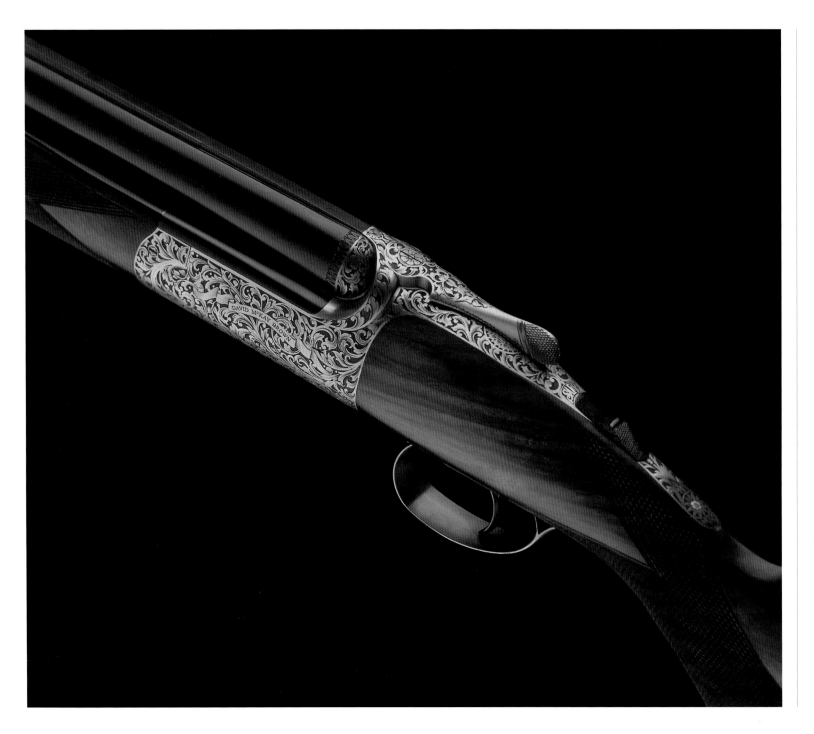

PLATE 21

David McKay Brown 12-bore Over/Under

McKay Brown's success with his Round Action over/under has undoubtedly helped inspire the current renaissance in British o/us. Aesthetically it has proven influential and is now widely imitated, particularly in Italy. Currently over/unders comprise the majority of McKay Brown's annual production.

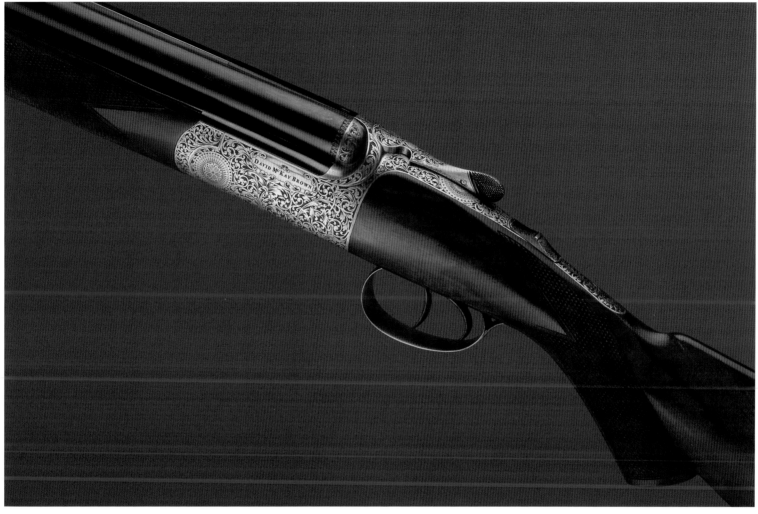

PLATE 22

David McKay Brown 12-bore Over/Under

McKay Brown remains a 'gunmaker' in the truest sense of the word, with his own
factory and in-house staff of craftsmen specially trained to make the Round Action.
This 12-bore over/under has 30-inch barrels, double triggers, and is engraved with
Scottish scroll. It weighs 7lb 4oz.

PLATE 23

David McKay Brown .470 Double Rifle

McKay Brown builds a handful of big-bore double rifles on the side-by-side Round Action design every year. The design's near-solid action makes it well suited for withstanding the stresses generated by dangerous-game calibres. This .470 has 25-inch barrels and was engraved by England's Martin Smith.

PLATE 24

David McKay Brown 20-bore Round Action

Smallbore side-by-sides – like this 20-bore with 29-inch barrels – comprise most of McKay Brown's sales to the United States, where grouse, woodcock and quail hunters prize them for their svelte lines and racy handling. This example has classic Scottish scroll over colour-case-hardened action.

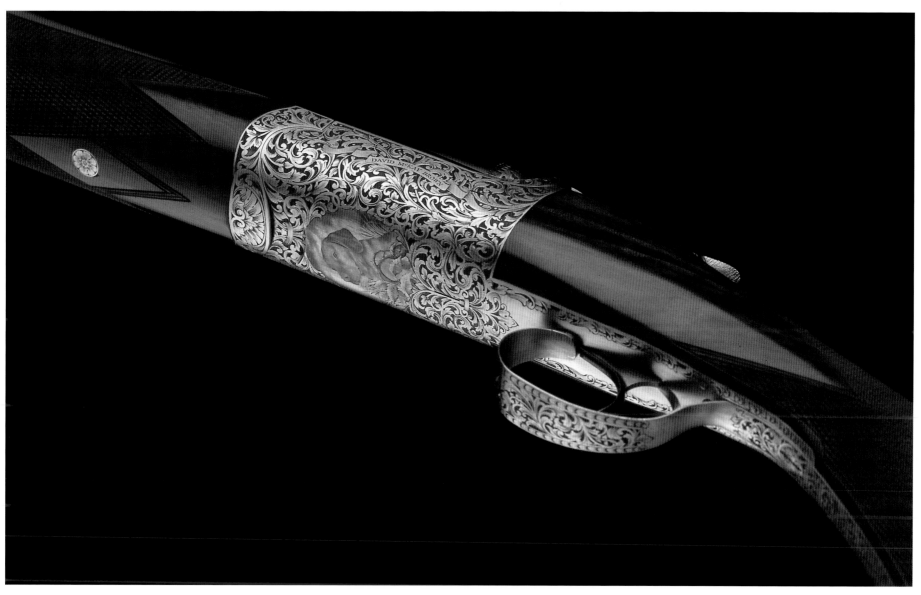

PLATE 25

David McKay Brown 12-bore Over/Under

This view of the underside of a Round Action over/under provides a perfect example of how the design got its name.

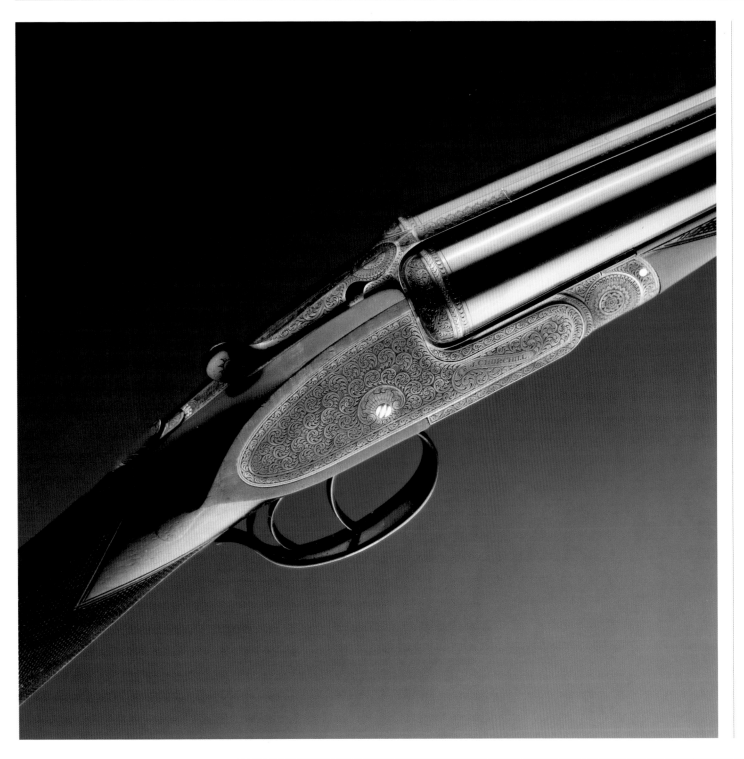

PLATE 26 *(left)*

E.J. Churchill 12-bore Sidelock

An E.J. Churchill 'Premiere' sidelock built in the late 1990s, made when the Churchill name was being revived by the owners and directors of West Wycombe Shooting Grounds. It has the pinless lockplates and full scroll engraving typical of this model – but not 'XXV' barrels, the latter made famous by Robert Churchill but since the eighties distinctly out of fashion.

PLATE 27 *(right)*

George Coster & Son Sidelock

This bar-action 12-bore sidelock by Glasgow's George Coster displays finely executed scroll and high-quality game scenes. Although it was probably partially or entirely built in Birmingham, its chopper-lump barrels, the clean sculpting of the action bar and fences, and lack of a top extension or a through-lump, reveals that it was made as a top-quality gun – quality typical of gunmakers throughout Scotland. Build date is unknown but was probably made in the mid-1920s.

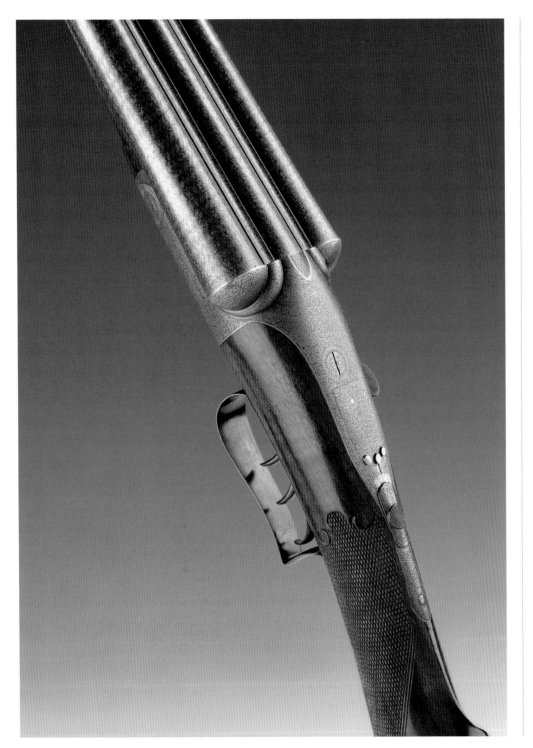

PLATE 28

John Dickson 16-bore Three-barrel Round Action

Edinburgh's John Dickson made a speciality of three-barrel guns – building something in the order of 27 in varying configurations. This 16-bore side-by-side-side 'Round Action' has three triggers and sidelever opening. Other variants had two triggers and toplever opening; yet others had the middle barrel above or below the outlying pair.

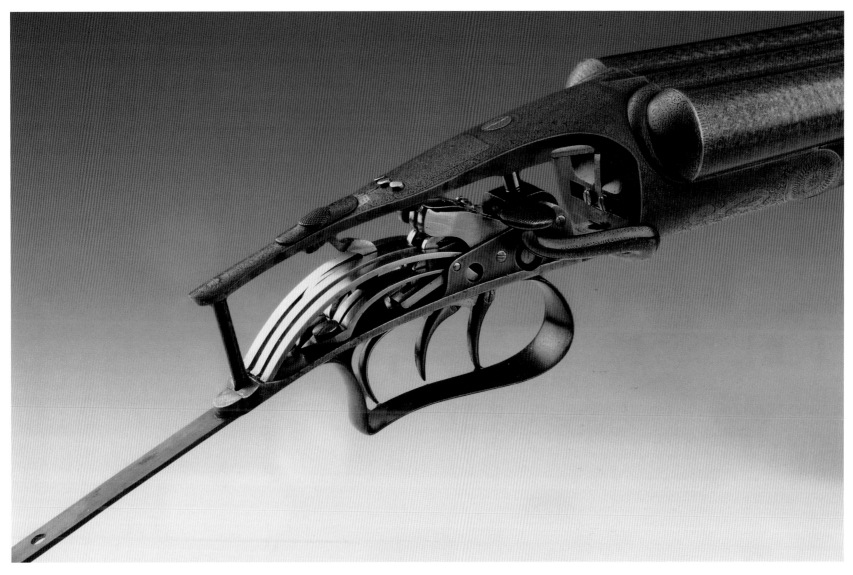

PLATE 29

John Dickson 16-bore Three-barrel Round Action sans stock

Shown without its stock, the triggerplate lockwork of this triple-barrel Round Action displays the high level of finishing and craft Dickson was known for. The design was patented in 1882.

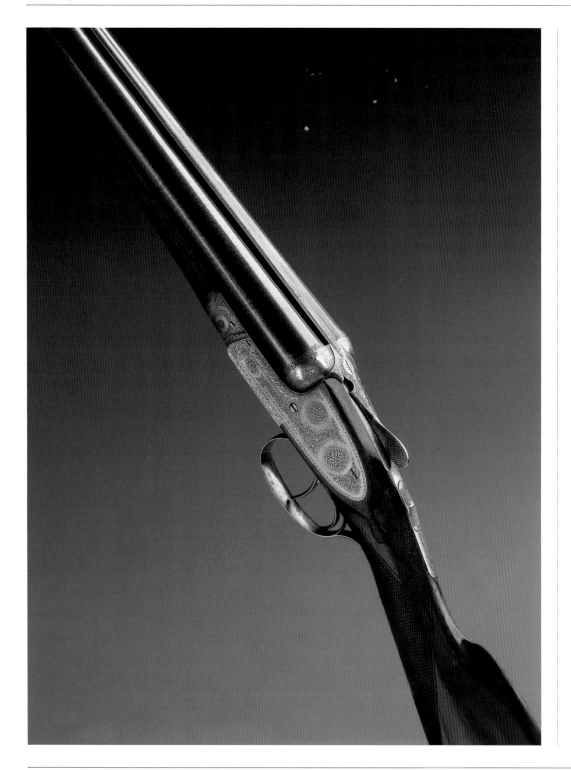

PLATE 30

John Dickson 12-bore Sideplated Round Action

Not all Dickson Round Actions were made round: this example was actioned and sideplated to resemble a sidelock – a disguised triggerplate gun, in essence. However, this Dickson retains the firm's characteristic toplever and top-safety shapes. While round actions, as well as best-quality boxlocks, have proven formidable competitors to sidelocks through the years, the latter's thoroughbred lines and extra areas for engraving area have prompted makers of the former to attempt imitation on numerous occasions – as evidenced here.

PLATE 31

John Dickson Hammergun

This Dickson hammergun was made with a Jones-type rotary underlever, and a round body with back-action locks. Although particularly sleek and elegant, it is also a strong design because the location of mainsprings behind the hammers leaves the action uncut.

PLATE 32

D.J. Dryhurst 12-bore easy-opening Sidelock

Before helping relaunch W.W. Greener, David J. Dryhurst was one of Britain's most respected gunmakers to the trade. He also built about twenty-five guns under his own name – such as this best-quality 12-bore Holland-type sidelock engraved with Alan Brown's classic iteration of game scenes and fine scroll. One of seven Dryhurst guns engraved by Brown, they were made between 1978 and 1984, and its quality and finish reveal why Dryhurst was picked to help build guns for some of London's most prestigious names. Note the elegant fences and the classic, clean sculpting of the flutes and action bar.

PLATE 33

William Evans 12-bore 'Extra Best' Sidelocks

This pair of best William Evans sidelocks was completed around 1915 to match a pair of guns built for the Duke of Connaught. Evans historically used a variety of outworkers to help build its guns, and its finest guns, like these illustrated would have passed through the hands of London's top craftsmen to the trade, John Robertson of Boss & Co. fame being a prime example. The Evans record books indicate these guns were built and finished to 'extra best quality' standards and they are distinguished by superbly rendered Evans-pattern bold scroll. Company records do not mention an engraver but the scroll's quality and fluid style harken to the workshop of London's Harry Kell.

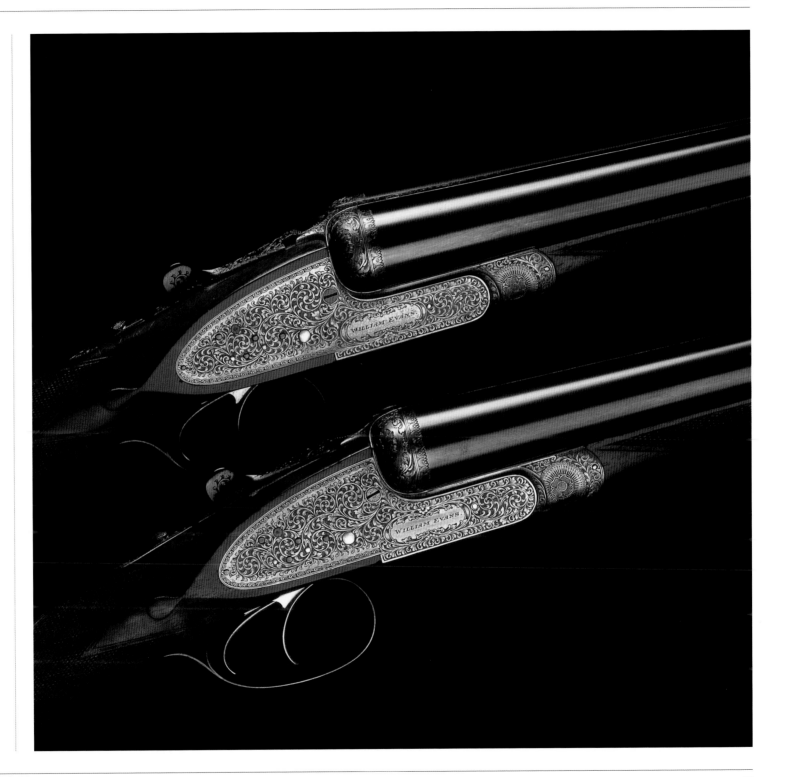

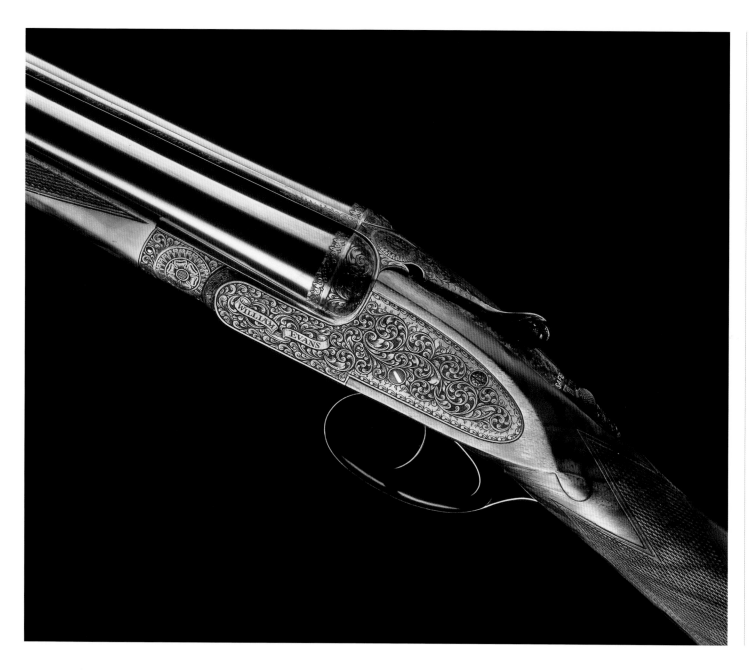

PLATE 34

William Evans 28-bore Sidelock

A 28-bore William Evans easy-opening sidelock completed in 2009, with engraver Andy Miles's interpretation of Evans's bold scroll over a colour-case-hardened action and 'pinless' lockplates. With 29 inch barrels and a $15^7/_8$ inch stock, it weighs 5lb 10oz.

PLATE 35

12-bore William Evans Sidelock

At 7lb, this 12-bore William Evans easy-opener was finished in 2009 as a wildfowler – an unusual configuration of a best London sidelock. It was commissioned by an avid waterfowler, and is built with a Holland-type semi-selective single trigger – a boon for cold-weather shooting. Evans' bold scroll surrounds game scenes – geese on the left lockplate and retriever on the right – by engraver Andy Miles.

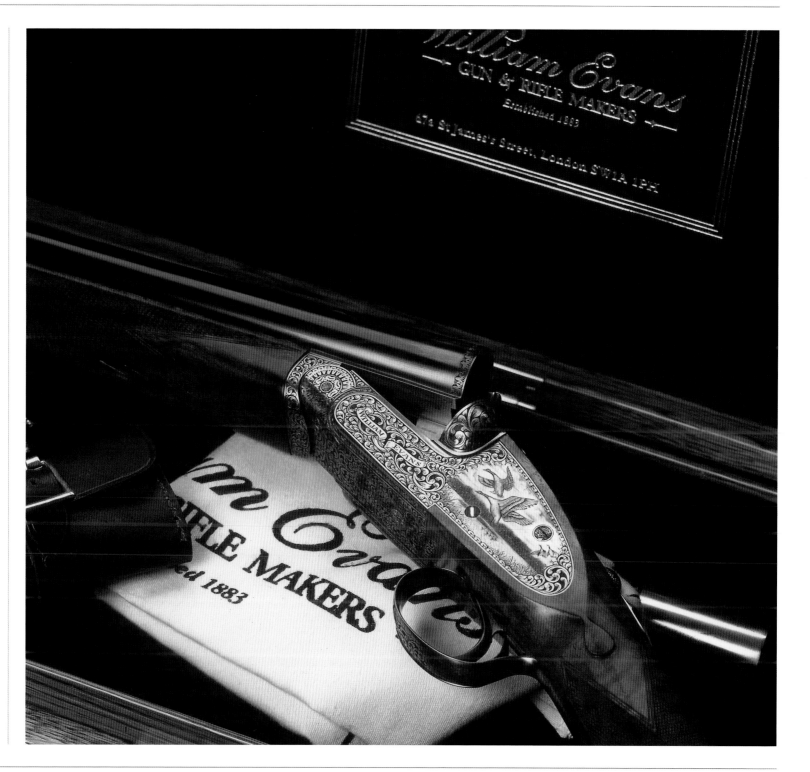

PLATE 36

Pair of William Evans Sidelock Ejectors

The pride of any shooting party, this pair of William Evans 12-bore easy-opening sidelocks was built in 1995 on Holland-type actions for one of the company's directors. They were engraved by Marcus Hunt, son of famed engraver Ken Hunt, and showcase Evans' bold scroll and game scenes framed by a twined border.

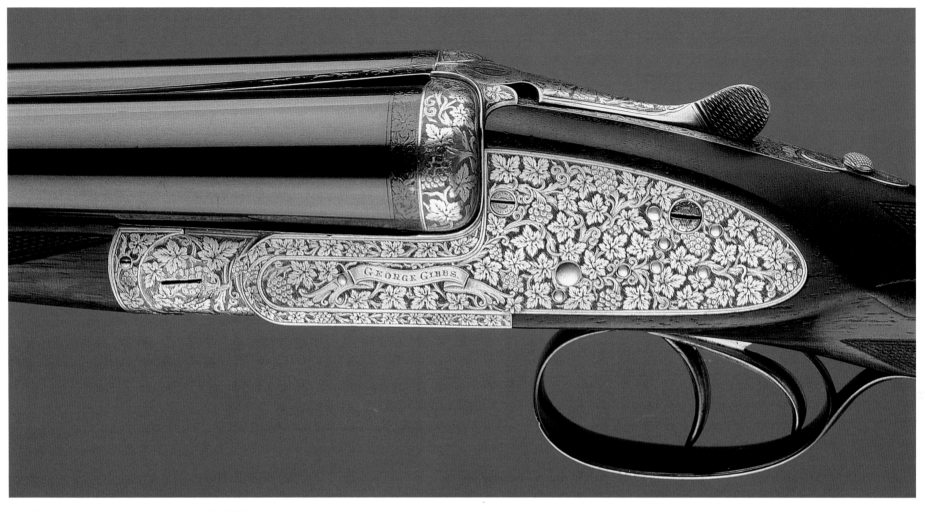

PLATE 37

George Gibbs Sidelock

This George Gibbs sidelock appears to be a London-pattern bar-action gun save for the 'fruiting vine' engraving favoured by a number of provincial gunmakers, Gibbs included. It was almost certainly engraved by Harry Morris, in Birmingham. As a riflemaker, Gibbs always preferred back-action locks, which can make for a stronger frame, even on its smoothbores. It was after the 1900s that the firm bowed to popular demand and began widely using London-style bar-action locks, as seen in this example.

PLATE 38

Stephen Grant 12-bore Sidelever Hammergun

This 12-bore sidelever Stephen Grant hammergun with back-action rebounding locks is built on Patent No. 251 of 31 January 1871, by E. C. Hodges. The triple-bite action is often referred to as the 'Grant & Hodges Patent' and Grant versions are often engraved as such. Long out of production, Atkin Grant & Lang are reviving the design with a new 20-bore Grant hammergun version, set to debut in 2010.

PLATE 39

Stephen Grant 12-bore Sidelever Sidelocks

A pair of sidelever Stephen Grants: a hammerless sidelock and a sidelever rounded-frame hammergun, the latter built on the 'Grant & Hodges Patent'.

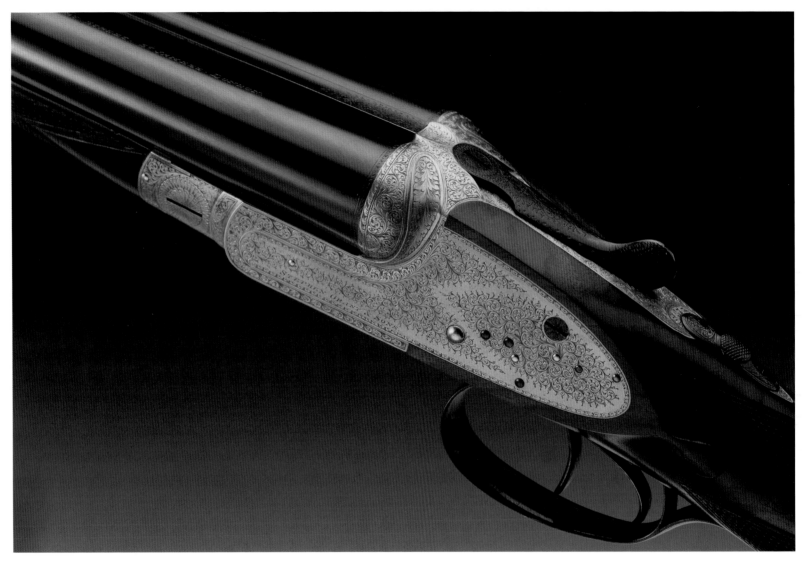

PLATE 40

Best 12-bore Stephen Grant Sidelock

Though best known for its sidelever sidelocks, Stephen Grant actually made more guns with toplevers, particularly in the decades following 1900. This sidelock was built about 1910, and has Southgate-type ejectors rather than earlier proprietary versions and is fitted with bar-action Chilton locks. It has fluted fences and sculpted action bar, and is decorated in the double-panel, fine-scroll pattern characteristic of Grant.

PLATE 41

Pair 12-bore Stephen Grant 'Lightweight' Sidelever Sidelocks

Two from a trio of special Stephen Grant best-quality 'Lightweight' model sidelocks built in 1936 for an English earl. They have the fluted fences and sidelevers typical of the maker, but also single triggers and are made on William Baker's '12/20' assisted-opening action. Records indicate they were embellished with scroll and game scenes in the workshop of noted London engraver Harry Kell.

PLATE 42

Quartet Stephen Grant 12-bore Sidelocks

A quartet of colour-hardened round-bodied Stephen Grant sidelocks completed in 2009, engraved with Boss-inspired rose and scroll. Sans the firm's characteristic fluted fences, they were built for an Austrian client with instructions to match his circa 1929 Boss. Made with 28-inch barrels by Bill Blacker, there were actioned by Gary Hibbert and stocked by Stephane Dupille.

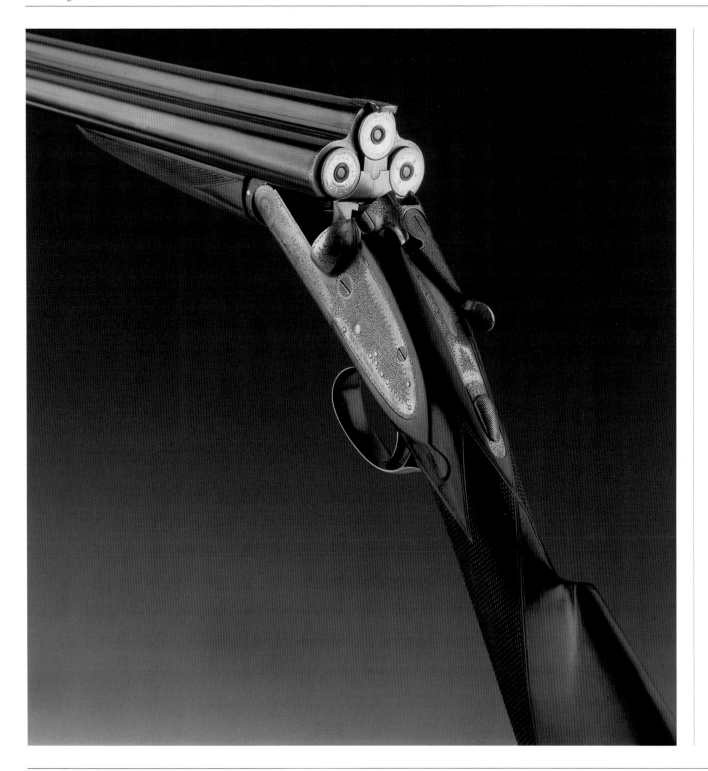

PLATE 43

Edwinson C. Green 12-bore Three-barrel, built for Lyon & Lyon

One of the marvels of early twentieth century British gunmaking was Edwinson C. Green's 1902-patent three-barrel gun with a non-selective single trigger, which normally fired the right barrel, centre, then left. Although a number of makers of the era produced triple-barrel guns as a means to advertise the reliability of their single triggers, Green seems to have produced its gun in earnest, with eighteen recorded as being made in 12-, 16- and 20 bores, with more thought to be extant. Several were built for Lancaster and Westley Richards, and this example was made for Lyon & Lyon, of Calcutta.

PLATE 44

W.W. Greener 12-bore 'St George' Sidelock

The 12-Bore 'St George' Sidelock, commissioned by Graham Greener and completed in 1992, helped relaunch the fortunes of W.W. Greener. Actioned by David Dryhurst and Richard Tandy, and engraved by Alan Brown with themes made famous by the firm a century ago on the original 'St George' guns, it was seen and subsequently purchased by one of the world's most influential collectors of modern sporting guns, who followed up with multiple orders for new exhibition-grade guns engraved by Britain's finest engravers. The resulting exposure has provided Greener with a full order book ever since.

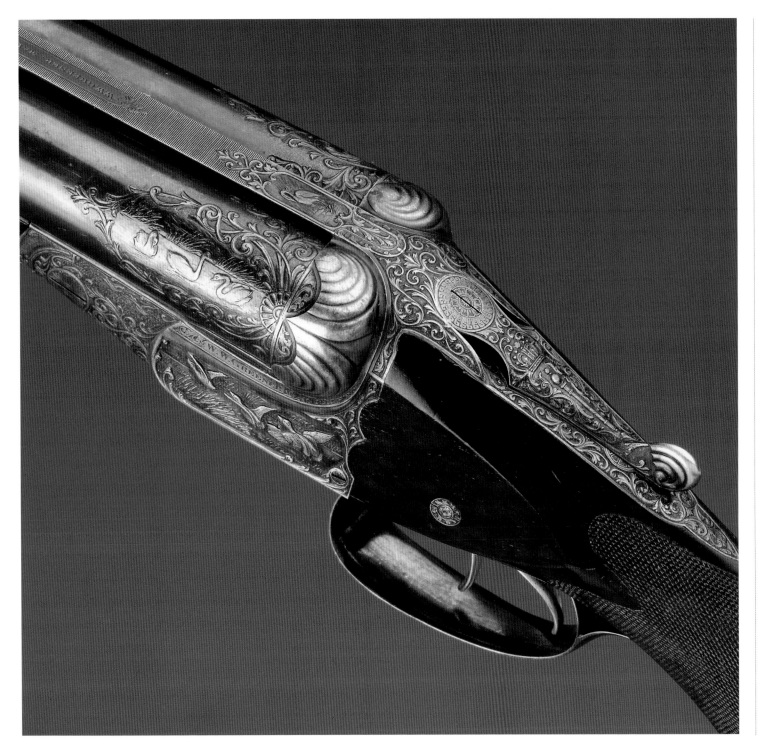

PLATE 45

W.W. Greener 8-bore Exhibition G-Grade

A big-bore 'G-Gun' – an exhibition 8-bore built in 1907 on the firm's proprietary 'Unique' hammerless ejector action. One of only a handful best-quality 8-bore Uniques ever made; it showcases sculpted and carved embellishment, including the seashell fences typical of the most expensive guns Greener's made during its historical heyday, with prices matching or exceeding the priciest guns made in London.

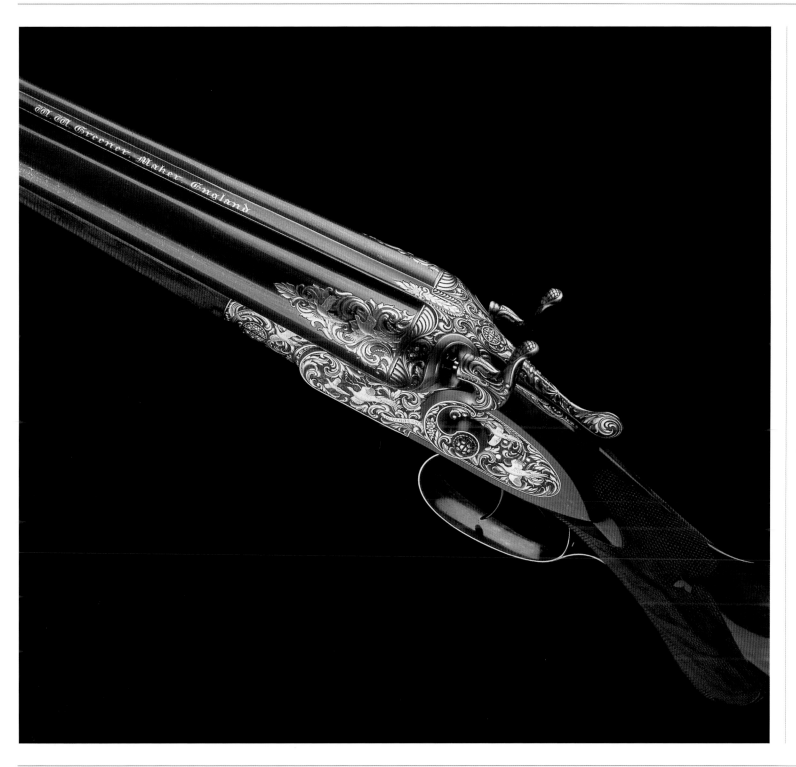

PLATE 46

W.W. Greener 12-bore Exhibition Grade Hammergun

Begun in 1889 and finished over a century later in 2007, this exhibition-grade Damascus-barrelled Greener hammergun may hold the record for the world's longest gun delivery time. It was originally actioned by 'Mr Camm' — during his day Greener's most experienced and talented actioner — then for reasons unknown put away unfinished in-the-white until David Dryhurst obtained it sixty years later from the Greener Museum Collection, which was in the process of being sold off to America. After thirty years in storage, it was actioned and finished by David Dryhurst and Richard Tandy, stocked by Peter Rowland, and engraved by Alan and Paul Brown — the latter incorporating Greener motifs into their engraving.

PLATE 47 *(left)*

W.W. Greener 12-bore 'St Louis II' G-Grade

One of two unfinished century-old 'Unique' actions was used by the Greener gunmaking team to create the 'St Louis II' gun, with embellishment by Alan and Paul Brown inspired by a pair of exhibition-grade G-Guns that took the gold medal at the 1904 World's Fair, held in the United States, in St Louis, Missouri. The engraving features carved seashell and foliate motifs, with gamebirds and gundogs inlayed in raised, carved gold.

PLATE 48 *(right)*

W.W. Greener 12-bore New 'St George' G-Grade

A second vintage 'Unique' action in-the-white was used to create a new St George – with engraving by Alan and Paul Brown to emulate W.W. Greener's most famous gun – the 'St. George Show Gun', originally built near the end of the nineteenth century to promote the firm's gunmaking skills. In addition to the proprietary action with self-contained ejectorwork, the new St George gun retains other historic signature features: Greener forend latch, intercepting sears based on Harry Greener's design, and a concealed crossbolt – meaning the bolt does not protrude through the side of the fence when the gun is opened. There are also horn inserts in the hand of the stock behind the action, an elegant horn forend tip, and Greener's distinctive fleur de lis chequering.

PLATE 49

W.W. Greener 12-bore Damascus-Barrelled Sidelocks

Using a store of vintage tubes David Dryhurst has collected since the 1960s, W.W. Greener has become the first British gunmaker to return damascus-barrelled shotguns to regular production – and in 12-, 16-, 20- and 28-bores. As of 2009, more than twenty-five new damascus guns have been completed or are under way. This damascus pair, a 12-bore *(right)* and a 28, completed in 2006, have Greener-pattern tight scroll over case-colour-hardened actions. Hand-carved Greener-style arcaded fences, double bars on the lower side of each barrel, horn-tipped forend, borderless chequering, and a wide-bow triggerguard with 'lay-back' rear trigger, help distinguish Greener sidelocks from London-pattern guns.

PLATE 50

W.W. Greener 20-bore 'G-Gun'

Built for James J. Baker, of America's National Rifle Association, this new scaled-frame 20-bore G-Gun was made on Greener's Facile Princeps action and has Boss-type ejectorwork. Built to the standards of a best sidelock, it has disc-set strikers and is also fitted with Harry Greener's patent intercepting safety sear — a costly and time-consuming feature to add within the confines of the gun's action. It also has a top safety, rather than the firm's characteristic side safety. The 'Four Seasons' engraving, by Brad Tallett, is based on a pattern originally developed by Greener's legendary Harry Tomlinson.

PLATE 51

W.W. Greener 12-bore New 'St George' G-Gun

Another view of the new St George – the third to be completed on a G-gun action. The original remains extant, though the second is believed to have been lost at sea shortly after its completion near the turn of the nineteenth century. Greener also returned the G-gun to limited production in the late 1990s, making them in 20- and 28-bore, and in .375 calibre as double rifles. The Facile Princeps action, on which the design is based, was used for new production, though the ejectors were based on the Boss system, rather than Greener's 'Self-Acting' or 'Unique' designs. The Boss ejector is similar to Baker design, which was used in Greener's 'Monarch' grade guns.

PLATE 52

W.W. Greener 12-bore Sidelock with interchangeable steel and Damascus Barrels

Built as a high-pheasant gun, this new Greener sidelock has interchangeable 32-inch barrels made of modern steel and also damascus, the latter built on unused vintage Greener 'best silver steel' tubes. Mechanically it is made with Greener-type forend latch and Harry Greener's 1914-patent lockwork with three-teardrop, five-pin bridles. Its fences have sideclips and arcades hand-carved by David Dryhurst. It was engraved by Phil Coggan, with the latter's interpretation of the firm's traditional 'four seasons' pattern which illustrates the shooting season as it progresses through fall into winter. Note the exposed Greener lockwork is not complete and is shown for illustration only, nor has the gun been hardened or final finished yet.

PLATE 53

Alex Henry Hammergun

This Alex Henry hammer rifle from the late nineteenth century is decorated with a variation of Celtic engraving – in this case inspired by Victorian artist Hubert Paton. Henry's hammer rifles were usually made to extremely high standards.

PLATE 54

Joseph Harkom Boxlock

Guns of Edinburgh's Joseph Harkom were invariably well made and the firm was especially noted for the superb quality of its boxlocks. This vintage boxlock exhibits lovely serpentine fences and carved action shoulders, tight scroll engraving, and excellent finishing. Note the sculpting, which extends through the top-lever. Many Harkom boxlocks will be found with gold-plated internal components.

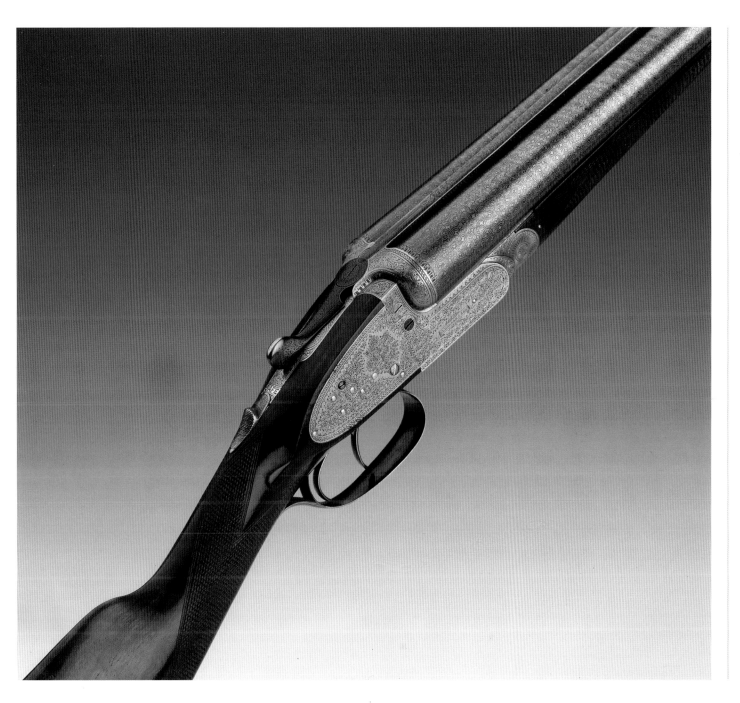

PLATE 55

Joseph Harkom Sidelock

Like the boxlock, this Harkom sidelock exhibits tight scroll engraving, beautiful damascus barrels, and elegant sculpting of the action bar. Company records have gone missing in the past through various changes of ownership and therefore precise identification and dating of this gun remains difficult. It is likely to have originated in Birmingham – note the top extension and it not being stocked to the fences – but it was probably finished out in the Harkom workshops. Unlike many Harkoms it has standard fences.

PLATE 56

Pair of Holland & Holland 12-bore Sidelock 'Royals'

Holland & Holland's 'Royal' is unquestionably the world's most-copied sidelock side-by-side – and with good reason. Mechanically it is relatively simple and supremely reliable, and Holland's bar-action design is attractive and adaptable to any number of external stylistic variations. This pair from 1990 is the classic iteration: square frames with fluted bars and beads and hand-detachable locks, engraved with Holland's house cutaway scroll on colour-case-hardened actions. Despite the increasing popularity of over/unders, sales at Holland over the last five years still average about two-to-one in favour of side-by-sides, a tribute to the Royal's enduring design.

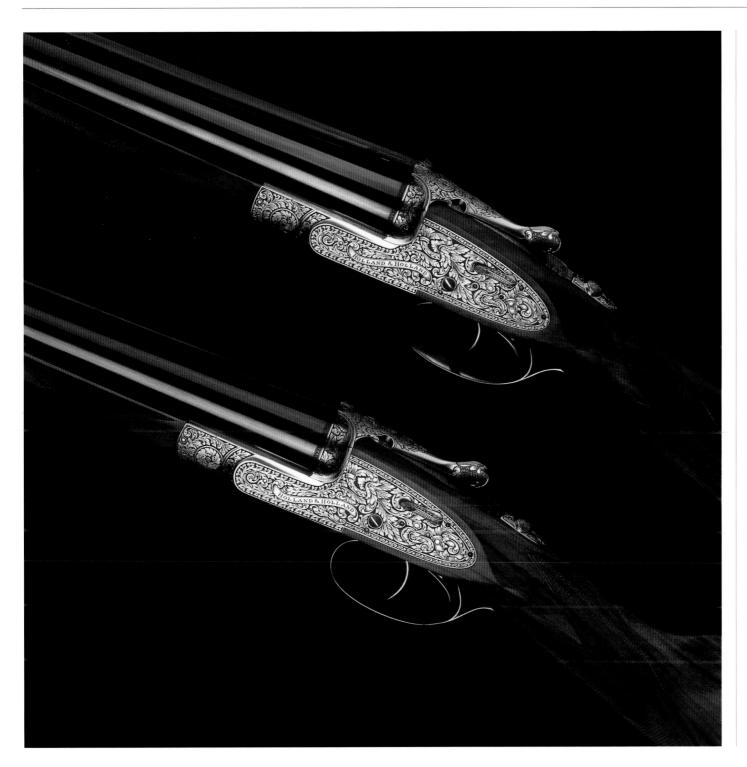

PLATE 57

Pair of Holland & Holland 12-bore Sidelock 'Royals'

Since the introduction of its signature cutaway scroll pattern in the 1890s – or 'Royal scroll' as the company calls it – Holland & Holland has been known for its flamboyant engraving patterns. This pair of 12-bore Royals built in 2000 and engraved in-house bears a modern interpretation of acanthus scroll.

PLATE 58

Pair of Holland & Holland 20-bore Sidelock Royals

Made in 2007, these 20-bore 'Royals' were engraved by Holland & Holland's Kirsty Swan and are adorned with scroll framing close-ups of the heads of Britain's game birds.

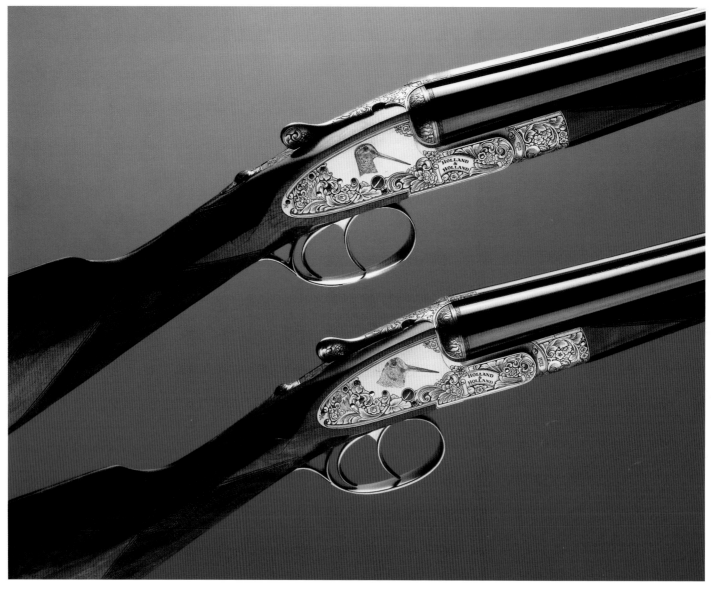

PLATE 59

Pair of Holland & Holland 20-bore Sidelock Royals

The right lockplates of the 'Royals' shown in plate 58 depict a
snipe *(top)* and a woodcock.

PLATE 60

Holland & Holland 20-bore Sidelock Royal

A 20-bore 'Royal', circa 2008, featuring Allan Portsmouth's carved fences and bold-scroll engraving, with vignettes on the locks and on the base of the frame depicting Victorian and Edwardian shooting scenes. Portsmouth, who currently works on his own, trained as an engraver at Holland & Holland under Ken Preater, and is particularly well known for his acanthus and scroll patterns.

PLATE 61

Holland & Holland .300 cal. Sidelock 'Royal' Double Rifle

Holland & Holland's rise to best gunmaker status in the late nineteenth century was in large part predicated on its forte for building (and regulating) double rifles, and also for its advances in rifle cartridge development. Like its shotgun cousin, Holland's 'Royal' double rifle still sets the world's design standard for sidelock side-by-side big-game rifles. This .300 calibre example was built in 2007 and was engraved in-house by Sam Faraway. Whereas the side-by-side 'Royal' shotgun employs bar-action locks, the rifle version use back-action locks, which adds strength to the frame.

PLATE 62

Holland & Holland .500/.450 Sidelock 'Royal' Double Rifle

With its 'Products of Excellence' series of the 1960s, 1970s and 1980s, Holland & Holland played a major role in promoting the rise of the modern British 'High Art Gun'. The series showcased the nation's finest gunmaking and engraving skills, and helped pave the way for emulators to follow. This .500/450 'Royal' double rifle follows in that tradition: it is the Theodore Roosevelt 1909–2009 Centenary of his original Holland & Holland .450/.500 'big stick'. Engraved by Phil Coggan with scroll and scenes from Roosevelt's safaris, it is part of Holland's 'African Hunter' commemorative series and was first exhibited at the 2009 Safari Club International Convention.

PLATE 63

Holland & Holland 12-bore 'Royal' Sidelock Over/Under

Holland's 'Royal' sidelock over/under is the third type of best o/u to be produced by the firm — and unquestionably its most successful. Introduced in 1992, it was the product of careful analysis of competing designs — with elements subsequently taken from them and prior H&H guns. Modern Continental designs that have proven robust inspired the new Royal's ejectors and single trigger, whereas its back-action locks and exterior sculpting remain classic Holland & Holland. The result is a reliable, best-quality British over/under that combines tradition and innovation in a single handsome design.

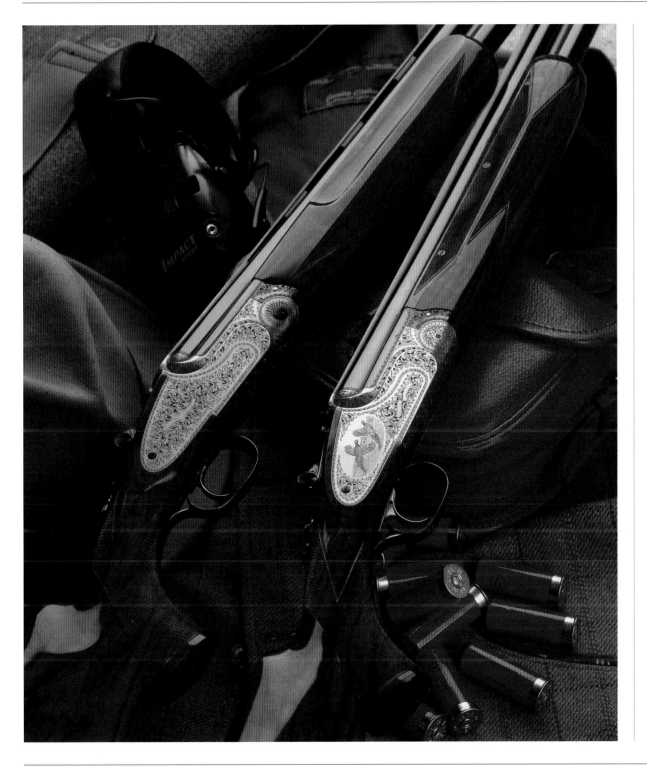

PLATE 64

Holloway & Naughton Britannia Over/Unders

Holloway & Naughton introduced the Britannia in 2006; a new design intended to be built to best English standards yet be durable enough to withstand intense, sustained shooting – and all brought to market at a cost substantially lower than its British sidelock over/under competitors. The gun pictured on the left is the sporting/high-bird model; on the right is the field/game model. The two versions share the same features, and average 7lb 8oz in weight, but the sporting version has thicker barrel-wall thickness (.035") compared to the field gun's (.028"). The Britannia was initially designed as a triggerplate gun, as pictured, but has since evolved to a true sidelock. Appearance-wise the two variations are almost identical, though the sidelock's lockplates are slightly rounder along the top and the triggerguard has a more pronounced bow.

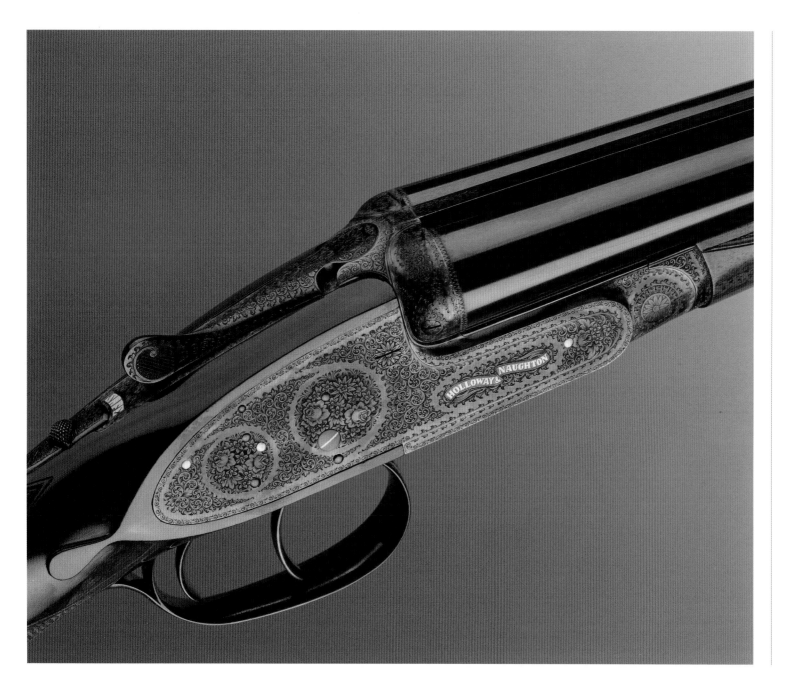

PLATE 65

Holloway & Naughton 28-bore 'Premier' Self-Opening Sidelock

Holloway & Naughton's new 'Premier' model sidelock self-opener, built on a Beesley-type action – this one as a 28-bore. This example was completed in 2007 and was engraved with fine rose and scroll by Belgium's Geofroy Delahaut. Holloway & Naughton introduced the Premier to its line in 2005, after eight years of development. It is available in .410 through 12-bores, all on scaled frames.

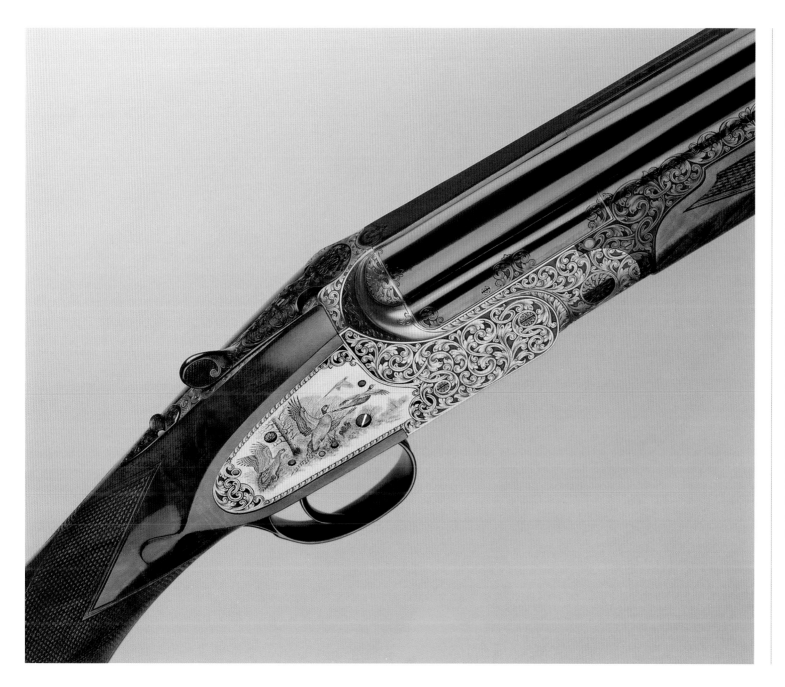

PLATE 66

Holloway & Naughton 12-bore 'Premier' Sidelock Over/Under

Holloway & Naughton's 'Premier' sidelock over/under is built on a true Boss-type action – a complex design made by only a handful of other best gunmakers. Holloway & Naughton's nod to modernity is its inertia-trigger, simpler than the original Boss design. This gun was built in 2004 and engraved in bold scroll and game scenes by Geofroy Delahaut. Delahaut was born in 1964, the son of Marie-Louise Magis, an engraver at Fabrique Nationale. He trained with Belgium's renowned Alain Lovenberg before setting up on his own.

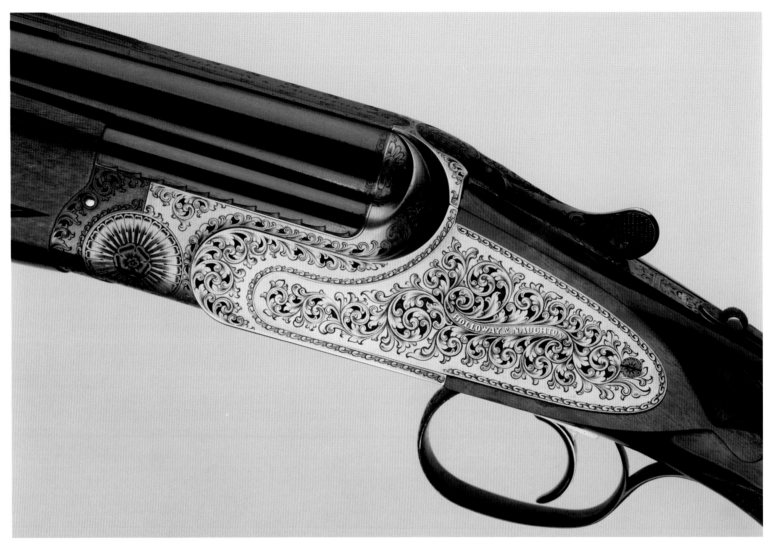

PLATE 67

Holloway & Naughton Britannia 12-bore Triggerplate Over/Under

A close-up of the Britannia. This is a triggerplate version; today Britannias are made as true sidelocks. In the course of production the company's Andrew Harvison found that building a high-quality triggerplate cost virtually as much to make in England as a sidelock, so the Britannia was redesigned. It is made with the same materials, engraving and level of finishing as the company's Premier; its somewhat simpler mechanical design helps lower the price.

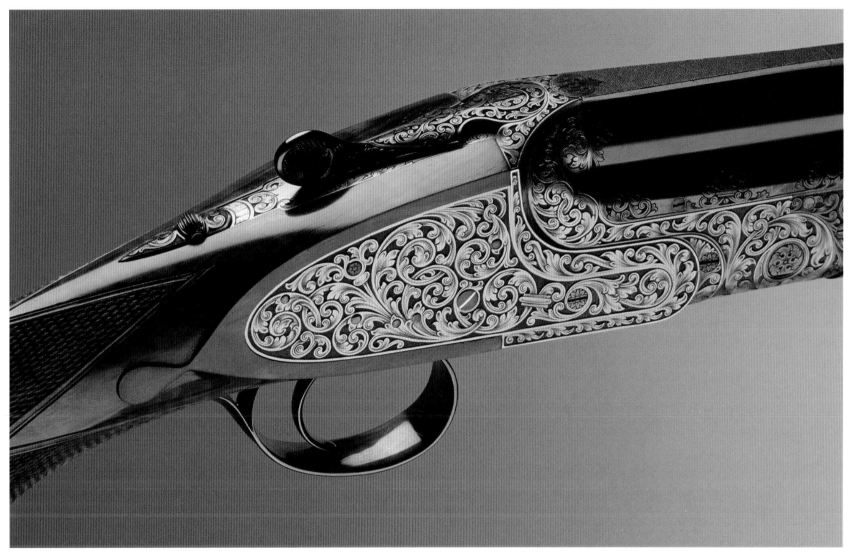

PLATE 68

Holloway & Naughton 20-bore 'Premier' Over/Under

A close-up of a smallbore Premier, also engraved by Geofroy Delahaut.
Like the side-by-side Premier, the Boss-type over/under was eight years in
development before entering production in 2003. It exhibits superb
finishing and stocking.

PLATE 69

William Palmer Jones
Three-barrel Hammergun

This William P. Jones hammergun, a 12-bore with a .360 barrel over the smoothbore tubes, showcases Patent No. 17732 of 1888 — a 'firing appliance' that allowed two hammers to fire three or four barrels. On the right hammer, note the moveable nose that can be pivoted to strike either the rifle barrel up top or the right shotgun barrel. Though ingenious, it does not appear to have been widely adopted in the trade — unlike his ubiquitous 'try gun' invention of 1889, a fixture at shooting schools to this day.

PLATE 70

Charles Lancaster
20-bore Four-Barrel

This damascus-barrelled 20-bore Lancaster is a late iteration of the various four-barrel gun designs company owner H.A.A. Thorn experimented with in the 1880s. The top barrels fired first – the front trigger for the right upper barrel and the rear trigger for the upper left. The Winchester-style underlever was used to cock the locks for the lower barrels. Usually built as 20-bores to control weight, Thorn's four-barrel guns were mechanically ingenious but never achieved great popularity in a shooting culture dominated by twin-barrel side-by-sides.

PLATE 71

Joseph Lang & Sons 12-bore Self-Cocking Hammergun

Although modern Italian gunmakers are today known for making 'self-cocking' hammerguns with top safeties, there is little new under the sun – or in sporting gun design. This Lang hammergun was made in June 1875 for one J.G. Starke, Esq., and was made on Edwin Hughes's Patent 1290 of same year. Hughes, then Lang's managing director, developed his push-forward underlever-cocking design to be built in both hammer and hammerless versions, and with either triggerplate or back-action lockwork. Though the precise version is not explicitly stated in Lang's record books, the rounded action and lack of pins in the lockplates strongly suggests this is the triggerplate incarnation. The lever not only cocked the gun but also withdrew the barrel-locking bolts.

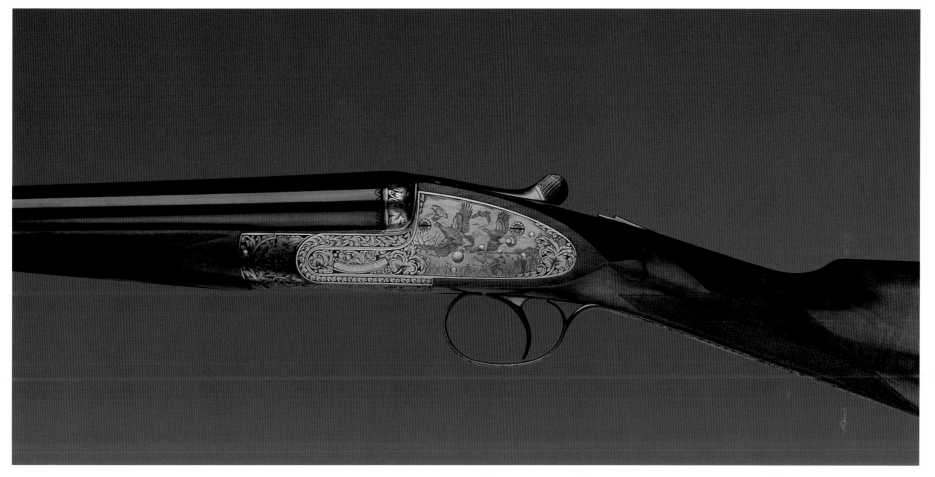

PLATE 72

Joseph Lang 20-bore Sidelock

This 20-bore Joseph Lang sidelock was completed in 2002. Fitted with 29-inch barrels, it has a single trigger to the modern Purdey design and was engraved with game scenes and scroll by Katia Filipovic. She was born in Liege and studied at the Leon Mignon school of gunsmithing and engraving, and today she lives in Grantham, Lincolnshire, where she engraves mostly for the British gun trade.

PLATE 73

J. Lang 'Twin Trigger' 12-bore Sidelock

A product of the era of single-trigger innovation, this 12-bore J. Lang sidelock was built in 1897 and was fitted with the 'Twin Trigger' design of Horatio Phillips – the latter an inventor and also an editor at *The Field*. The 'Twin Trigger' was actually a stacked double trigger fitted with a device to prevent double discharge should both triggers be pulled simultaneously. The inventor claimed it allowed the shooter to easily fire each barrel without relaxing the grip on the hand of the stock. Although it worked, it never caught on and examples so fitted are very rare.

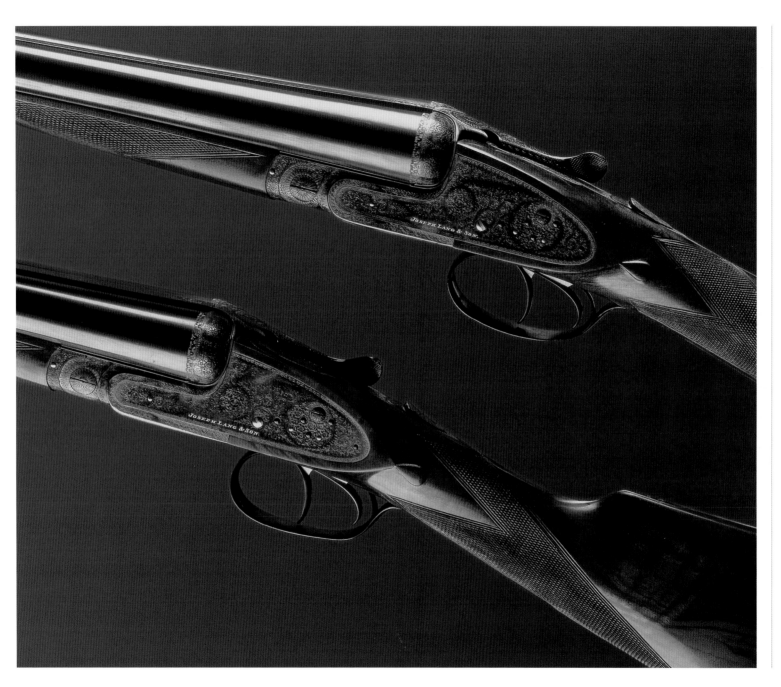

PLATE 74

Restored Pair 12-bore Joseph Lang & Sons Sidelocks

Ken Duglan's team of craftsmen at Atkin Grant & Lang restored this pair of Joseph Lang 'Imperials' in 2008. They were restocked by Stephane Dupille, with new barrels made by Bill Blacker jointed in by Gary Hibbert. New components were fitted and finished by Carl Russell and Alan Bower. The engraving is original, except for the maker's name picked out in gold, and the action was re-colour-hardened by Birmingham's Richard St Ledger. Reliable bar-action locks and simple Southgate-type ejectors make Lang sidelocks of this type excellent candidates for full restoration.

PLATE 75

G.E. Lewis 4-bore Damascus-Barrelled Sidelock

G.E. Lewis owner John Harris completed this massive 4-bore sidelock with damascus barrels in 1999 to commemorate the new millennium. Sporting 42-inch barrels and weighing 25lb, it was built on a Holland-type action by the special commission of a customer who had located a set of unfinished 4-bore damascus tubes, likely at least a century old. John Beech engraved the massive action – which was made from a solid forging – with cutaway scroll surrounding game scenes of geese. One lockplate depicts geese departing to symbolise the end of the century; the other shows geese arriving to ring in the new one. Despite its size, the action and stock are beautifully proportioned. The barrels were blacked rather than browned; Harris said he did this to give the gun a more 'modern' look.

PLATE 76

George MacFarlaine 20-bore Three-Barrel

Although three- and four-barrel guns were produced by a number of makers in the Victorian era, George MacFarlaine revived the concept with a number of three-barrel guns he built in the 1990s. Guns were made on barrelled-actions sourced in Ferlach, Austria, but with McFarlaine's modifications and input. This 20-bore has a Purdey underbolt and a doll's-head top extension, and was engraved by Phil Coggan. Engraver Alan Brown executed the carved borders of the chequering. Boehler steel was used in the tubes to allow thinner barrel-wall thicknesses, thus minimising weight and promoting livelier handling.

PLATE 77

George MacFarlaine
10-bore Three-Barrel

MacFarlaine's first multi-barrel
project was a 10-bore three-barrel
built on Ferlach-machined frame
with Boehler-steel tubes, with
McFarlaine fitting and regulating
the components. It remains in his
family's possession.

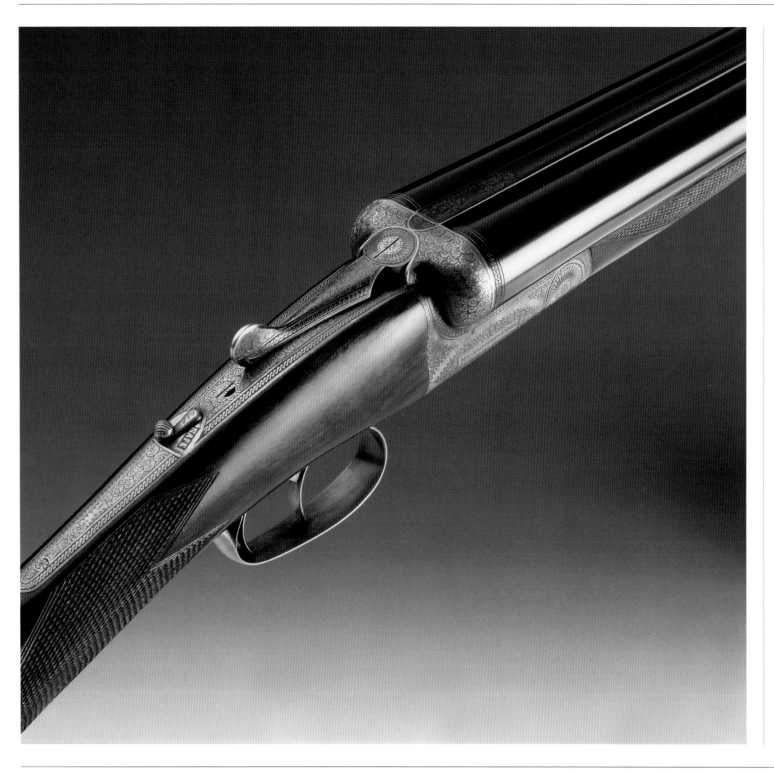

PLATE 78

James MacNaughton 12-bore Round Action Triggerplate

MacNaughton's 'Edinburgh Gun' is one of the most influential designs ever in British gunmaking – and is certainly Scotland's. Patented in 1879, it preceded John Dickson's first attempt at a triggerplate by a year. There are a number of early variants of MacNaughton's design but the principal two are made on a 'skeletal' (or bar-in-wood) action or with a 'solid' action, the latter shown here. The earliest guns cocked via an extra-long toplever but this gun has a conventional lever and is cocked with the fall of the barrels. It also exhibits MacNaughton's distinctive swivel safety, fine scroll engraving with twined-rope borders, and the svelte lines for which Scottish Round Actions are famous.

PLATE 79

John Manton 17-bore Flintlock Fowler

A single-barrel 17-bore flintlock fowler by London's John Manton, circa 1806. The gun incorporates a Manton-patent flintlock breech design and is sparingly engraved per the style of the period, most likely by London's William Palmer. Though less well known than brother Joseph, John Manton was a highly regarded maker in his own right, and was especially noted for his pistols and single-barrel fowlers.

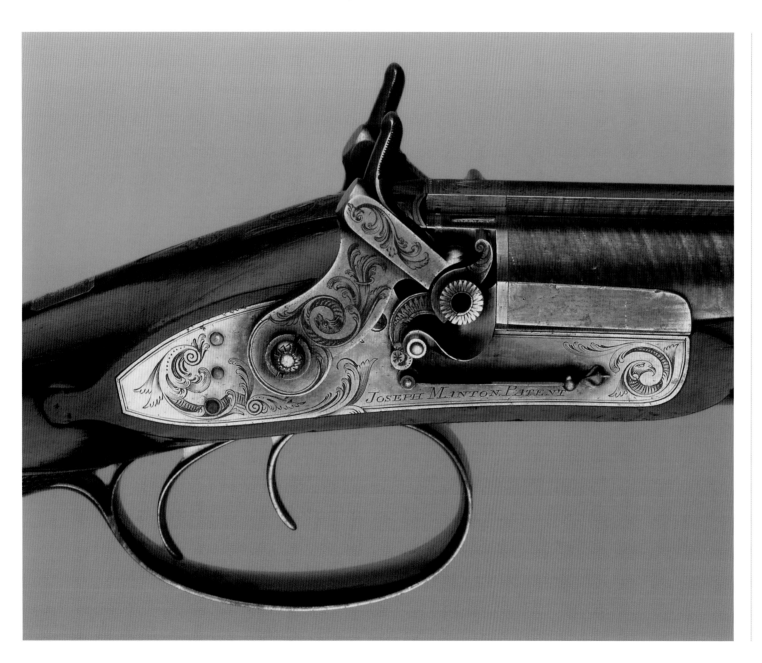

PLATE 80

Joseph Manton 14-bore Double Tube-lock

This Joseph Manton 14-bore 'tube-lock' double dates to 1821, and was made three years after Manton introduced the design. As a primer the tube-lock used a thin copper tube packed with fulminate of mercury, with one end of the tube inserted in the vent of the gun and the other placed upon an anvil made as part of the lockplate. The tube was held in position by a spring clip. When the hammer fell, the tube exploded, with the flash detonating into the vent to fire the charge. The tube-lock remained in use till the end of the percussion era and is considered one of Manton's many successes in advancing the craft of gunmaking.

PLATE 81

Accoutrements by Mike Marsh

Hand-crafted turnscrews and accoutrements by Mike Marsh grace the cases of many
of Britain's best gunmakers. Inspired by nineteenth century designs, Marsh works with
traditional materials and produces his accessories in-house in his own workshop.

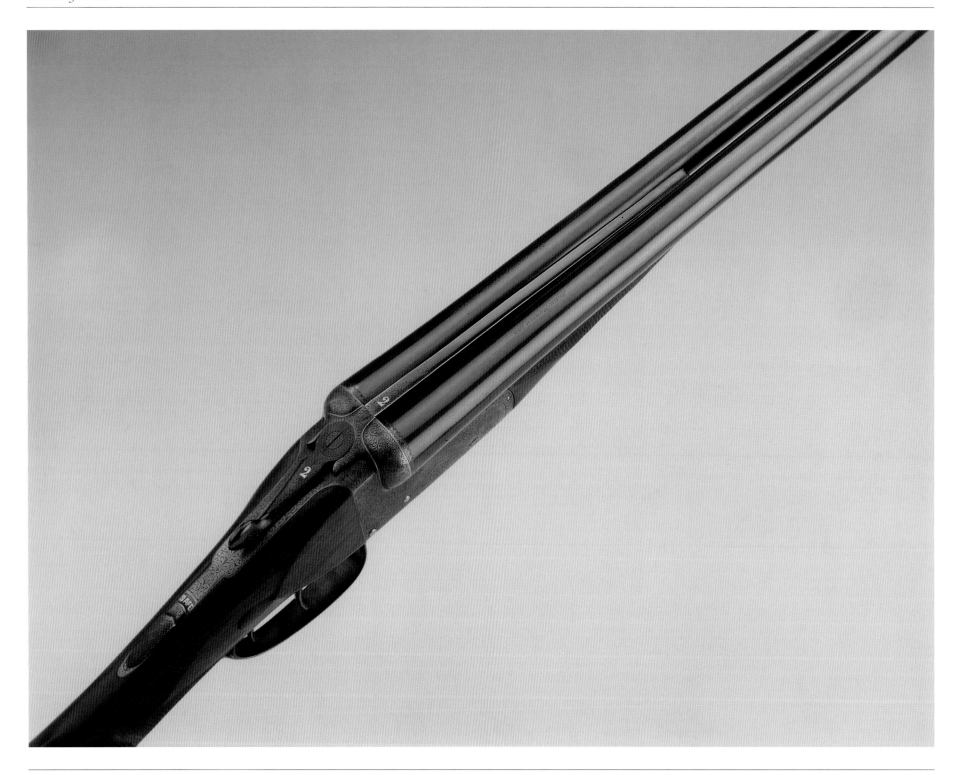

PLATE 82 *(left)*

Alex Martin Ribless Boxlock

The Scottish Alex Martin 'Ribless' isn't actually ribless – it lacks top and bottom ribs between a short swamped rib at the breech and a spacer at the muzzles. Designed to shave about a quarter-pound of weight off the front end, it promoted a fast-handling gun ideal for rough shooters and Martin's name became inextricably linked with the concept. Many were built by A.A. Brown & Sons, in Birmingham, like this example. Most were made as Anson & Deeley boxlocks, but some as sidelocks.

PLATE 83 *(right)*

Alex Martin Celtic-engraved Sidelocks

In addition to rifles and 'ribless' guns, Alex Martin was noted for its Celtic-engraved sidelocks. This pair exhibit fine interlacing strap and knotwork and mythical, dragon-like beasts, inspired by Medieval Celtic manuscripts. As author Douglas Tate writes in *British Gun Engraving*, the pair was, ironically, almost certainly made and engraved in Birmingham. Identical engraving can be found on some other Scottish makers, such as Alex Henry.

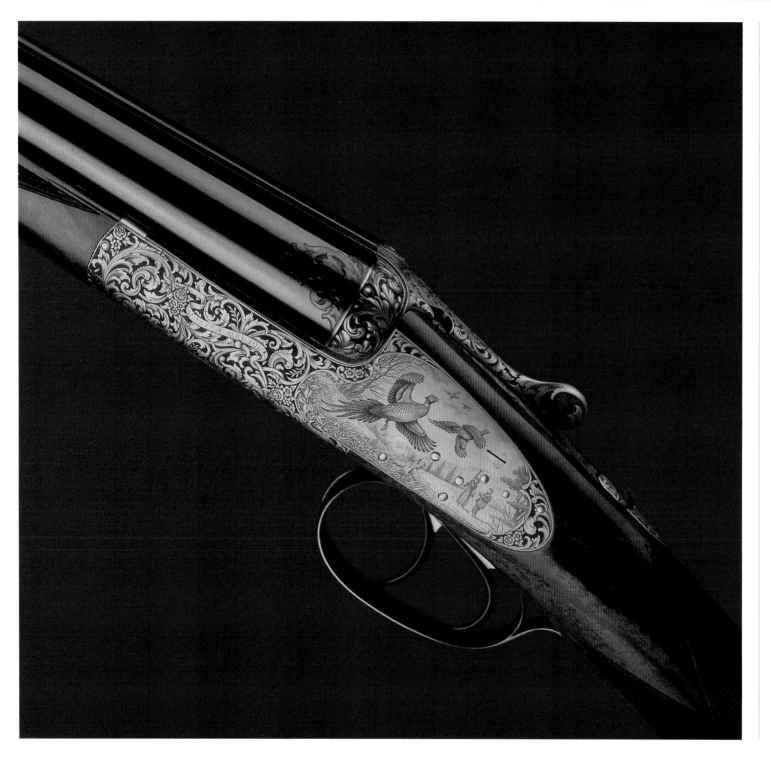

PLATE 84

P.V. Nelson 20-bore Sidelock

This P.V. Nelson 20-bore, one of a pair made for a lady, is built on a Boss-type rounded action. It was engraved by Alan and Paul Brown with chiselled fences, boldly cut scroll, and fine-line game and shooting scenes – some of the latter based on photographs of the client shooting in the UK.

PLATE 85

P.V. Nelson 20-bore Sidelocks

Two P.V. Nelson 20-bores from a three-gun set depicting Scottish game birds (the third, not shown, engraved with black grouse). Built on rounded-body Beesley/Purdey self-openers, they were made to complement a set of 12-bore guns engraved by Alan and Paul Brown.

PLATE 86

P.V. Nelson 12-bore Sidelock

Master engraver Ken Hunt embellished Nelson's rounded-body 12-bore Boss-type gun with waterfowl and foliage in multi-coloured gold inlays against a colour-case-hardened background.

PLATE 87

P.V. Nelson 20-bore Sidelock

Peter V. Nelson's 20-bore 'Renaissance Gun' is built on a rounded-bar Beesley self-opening action and is another showcase of the 'High Art' engraving typical of Alan and Paul Brown's work today. Deeply carved rococo scrollwork and scenes from Classical mythology dance over a stippled gold background.

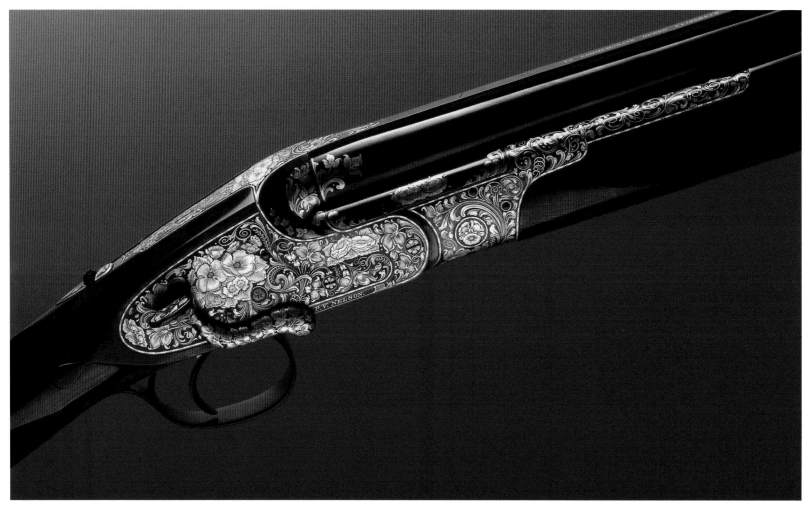

PLATE 88

P.V. Nelson 20-bore Sidelever Sidelock Over/Under

Nelson's 20-bore 'Jubilee Gun' was completed in 2002 – and so named for Queen Elizabeth's Golden Jubilee of same year. It is mechanically unique – a true Boss-type action but built with a sidelever. The floral design was embellished by Phil Coggan, and features flowers from the English countryside in raised damascene and flush multi-coloured gold. With 28-inch barrels it weighs only 5lb14oz. Nelson actually built it for himself, rather than on commission. Grant's photo of the gun graces the cover of Nigel Brown's *British Gunmakers Volume Three*.

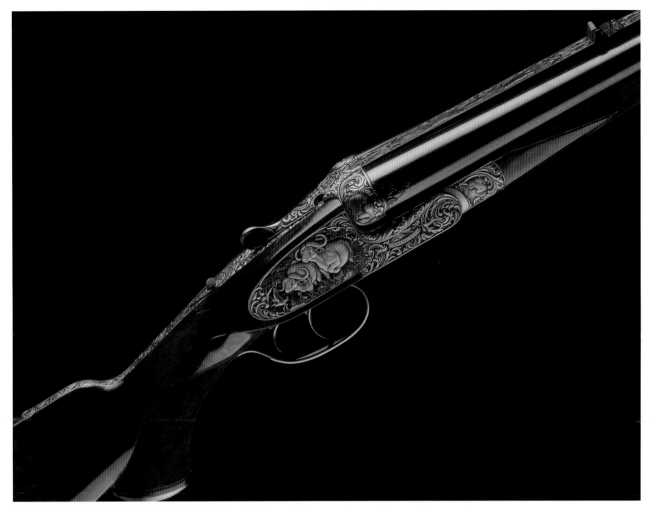

PLATE 89

P.V. Nelson .375 Sidelock Double Rifle

One of four from the recently completed 'Legacy Set' this .375 double rifle was built on a Boss-type action but with Holland-style bolsters, sideclips and a third bite. Nelson's most important client conceived of the set as a way of showcasing the gunmaker's illustrious career and the four principal designs upon which he made during it – the double rifle as pictured, Beesley/Purdey-type side-by-side gun, the Boss-type side-by-side gun, and the Boss-type over/under. For double rifle the .375 was chosen because it allows guns to be made, in the words of the client, 'proportionately about perfect'. Alan and Paul Brown carved the gun, with buffalo on the right lockplate.

PLATE 90

P.V. Nelson .375 Sidelock Double Rifle

Fighting lions carved by Alan and Paul Brown adorn the left lockplates of Nelson's .375 double rifle built for his Legacy Set. The set is showcased in a magnificent oak chest built by Vince Rickard, with ebony accents and inlays of walnut. Another impetus for building the set was the client's possession of four perfectly matched blanks of exhibition-grade walnut, a rarity in gunmaking. The rifle is number four in the set.

PLATE 91

P.V. Nelson 28-bore Sidelock

Gun number three in the Legacy Set, this 28-bore was made on a Beesley/Purdey action. Note its utterly perfect proportions; no easy task for Nelson to achieve on a smallbore of this action type. Ken Hunt engraved the quail, pointing dogs and foliage in multi-coloured gold, an engraving style he has pioneered and perfected over his long career.

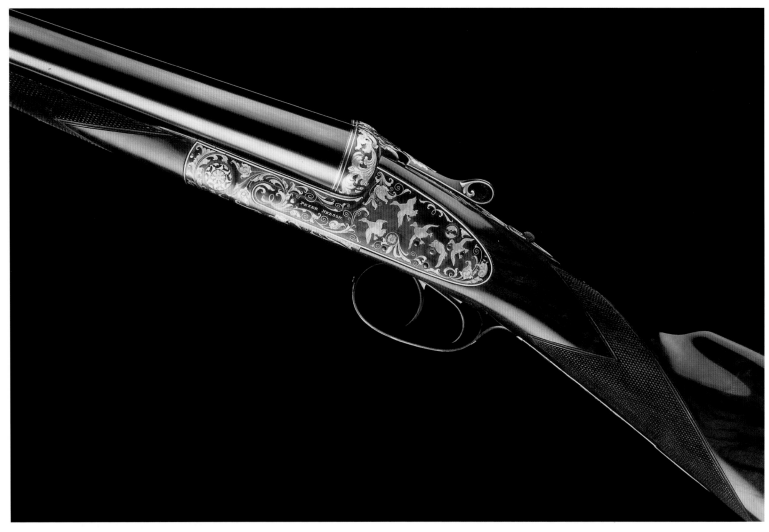

PLATE 92

P.V. Nelson 12-bore Sidelock

A round-bodied Boss-type action was chosen as the first gun of Nelson's Legacy Set, this example made in 12-bore. Phil Coggan inlayed highly detailed ducks and foliage in gold against a case-coloured background. Despite the flat inlays, the waterfowl possess a three-dimensional quality — and a sense of movement and drama — a tribute to the engraver's skills. The Browns, Hunt and Coggan were picked for the set because, in the client's words, 'I have always considered these the best engravers that ever lived'.

PLATE 93

P.V. Nelson 20-bore

A 20-bore Boss-type over/under was the second gun type for Nelson's 'Legacy Set'. Though the carving on stippled gold background by Alan and Paul Brown is of museum quality, it should not overshadow the skilled gunmaking — the true Boss over/under action has only been mastered by a handful of makers, and Nelson was one of the first to revive it. The type of engraving for the guns in the set was based on the styles each engraver is renowned for.

PLATE 94

P.V. Nelson 'Lord Nelson' Sidelocks

Peter V. Nelson's first gun dedicated to namesake Vice Admiral Horatio Lord Nelson helped launch his career as an independent gunmaker more than two decades ago and the second 'Nelson Gun', completed in 2009, marks a fitting tribute to his illustrious career. The initial gun, built as an exhibition piece on a 12-bore Beesley/Purdey self-opening action, was engraved by Phil Coggan with themes from the Battle of Trafalgar. The new sister gun has Coggan's scenes from the Battle of the Nile, where Nelson annihilated a French fleet in 1798. Top safeties are carved in the shape of mortars, and the furniture is decorated with period nautical themes. Both the 'Trafalgar' and 'Nile' guns exhibit the craftsmanship and attention to detail that has made P.V. Nelson the gunmaking equivalent of Britain's greatest admiral.

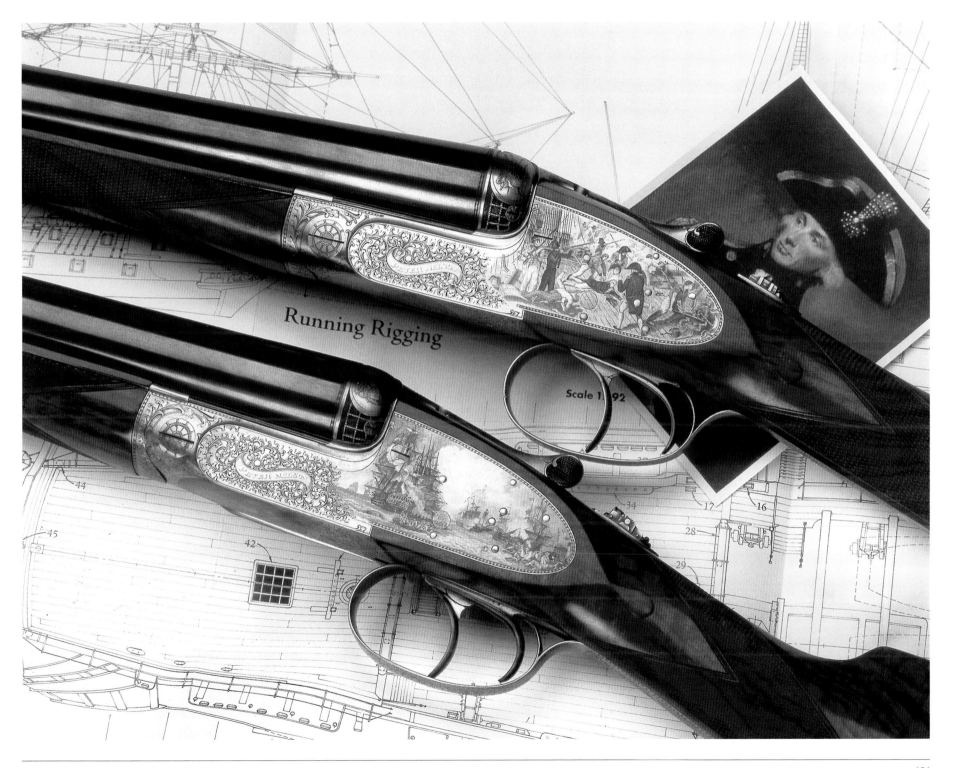

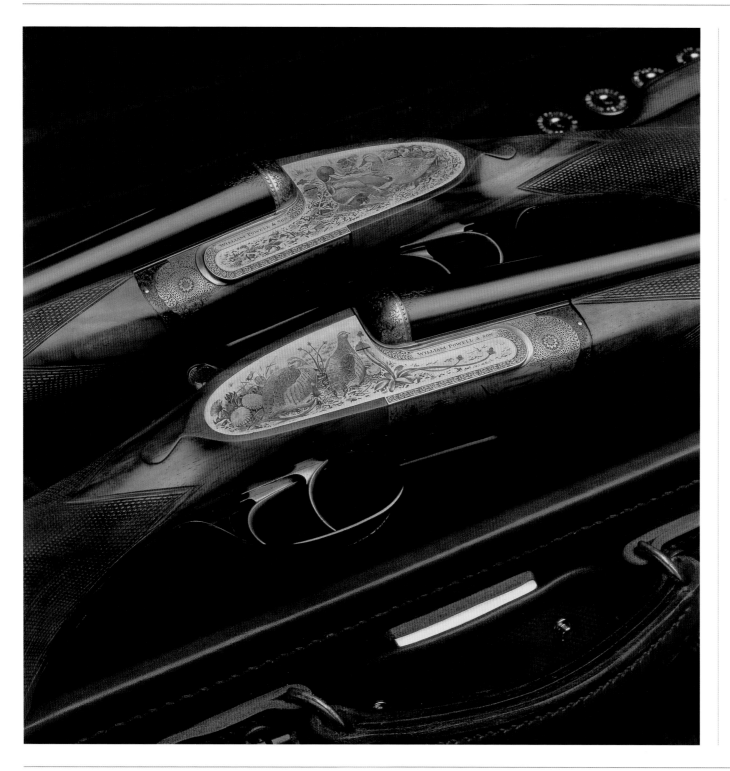

PLATE 95

Best 12-bore Sidelocks by William Powell & Sons

David Grant's image of this iconic pair of William Powell best sidelocks has graced the firm's mail-order catalogue for many years, and was also featured on the cover of Nigel Brown's *British Gunmakers Volume Two*. Actioned and finished by Bob Turner and completed in December 1992, they feature stunning game-scene engraving by Alan Brown based on artwork by Rodger McPhail. Bearing 30-inch chopper-lump barrels these 12-bore assisted openers were originally commissioned with Montecarlo stocks with pistol-grips and palm swells. Robin Brown, of A.A. Brown & Sons, purchased them second-hand in 2008 and converted the stocks to conventional game-gun design with Prince of Wales grips and they currently reside with a proud new owner in the north of Britain.

PLATE 96

William Powell Bar-in-Wood Hammergun

This Powell bar-in-wood hammergun features several of the firm's most important patents – Patent No. 1163 of 7 May 1864 and No. 1055 of 7 April 1869. The former is the 'lift up' snap-action and the latter are retracting strikers. It also bears Powell's distinctive 'thumb-print' carved fences. According to Peter Powell, it was likely built circa 1875. Its novel patents – and elegance – provide a good example of why Powell became one of Birmingham's most esteemed retail makers.

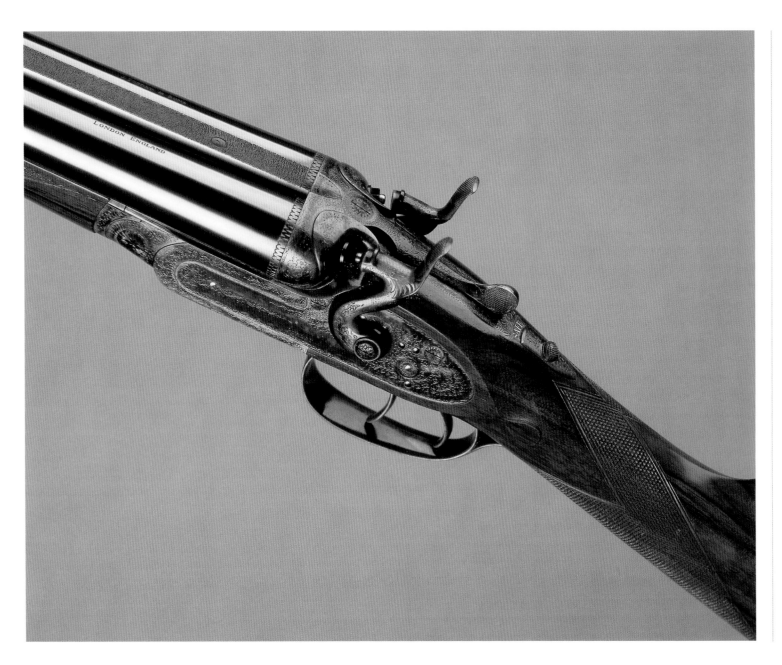

PLATE 97

James Purdey & Sons 12-bore Bar-in-Iron Hammergun

Encouraged by America's Griffin & Howe, Purdey reintroduced hammerguns to its line in 2001 – making them the first made by the firm since the early 1930s. Based on a circa 1923 bar-in-iron example, it was initially made in 12-bore with scaled-frame 20-bores announced in 2006. The basic design features percussion-style fences, low-profile hammers with rebounding locks, Southgate-type ejectors, Scott toplever and Purdey bolt – in other words, a best London hammergun at the apex of its technical development. This colour-hardened 12-bore was completed in 2009, weighs 6lbs 12oz, and was engraved in 'Purdey standard fine' rose and scroll by Martin Bublick.

PLATE 98

James Purdey & Son Ultra-Round Bar 28-bores

Left side of one gun from a pair of 28-bore ultra-round bar guns by James Purdey & Sons, completed in 2003 and engraved by Phil Coggan. Raised and carved quail peer from raised leaves against a backdrop of flush inlays of multi-coloured gold.

PLATE 99

James Purdey & Son Ultra-Round Bar 28-bores

The right side of the 28-bore pictured in Plate 98. This time Coggan's quail flush into a swirl of golden hues highlighted in silver.

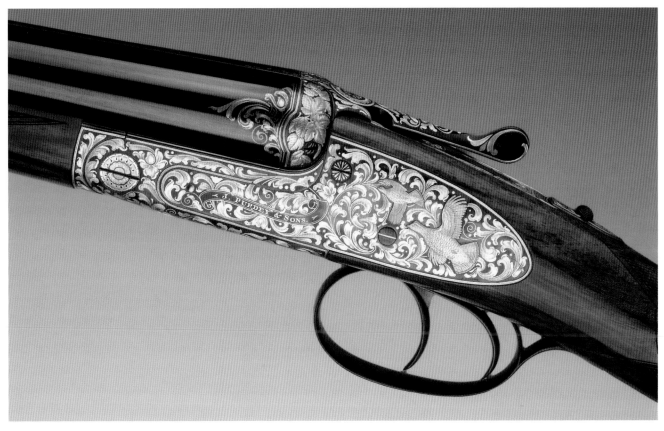

PLATE 100

James Purdey & Son Ultra-Round Bar 28-bores

The second gun of Phil Coggan's gold-embellished pair of Purdey 28s; the first pictured in Plates 98 and 99. This scene features flushing ruffed grouse – the 'king' of American upland game birds. Pinless lockplates provide an unblemished canvas for Coggan's multi-coloured gold inlays.

PLATE 101

James Purdey & Sons 'Sporter' 12-bore Over/Under

Announced in 2006, the triggerplate 'Sporter' is the first new gun design for Purdey of the twenty-first century, and is currently in production in 12- and 20-bores. Chairman Nigel Beaumont, along with Stephen Murray and Ian Clarke, re-engineered and improved a Perazzi-type action, and the firm is making all of the Sporter's major components in-house at its London factory at Felgate Mews in Hammersmith. The monoblock barrels and components are assembled by Perugini & Visini in Italy, with the bold-scroll house pattern executed by Creative Art. Then the Sporter returns to Felgate Mews for regulating, finishing and London proof. This example was completed in 2009 and weighs 7lb 10oz.

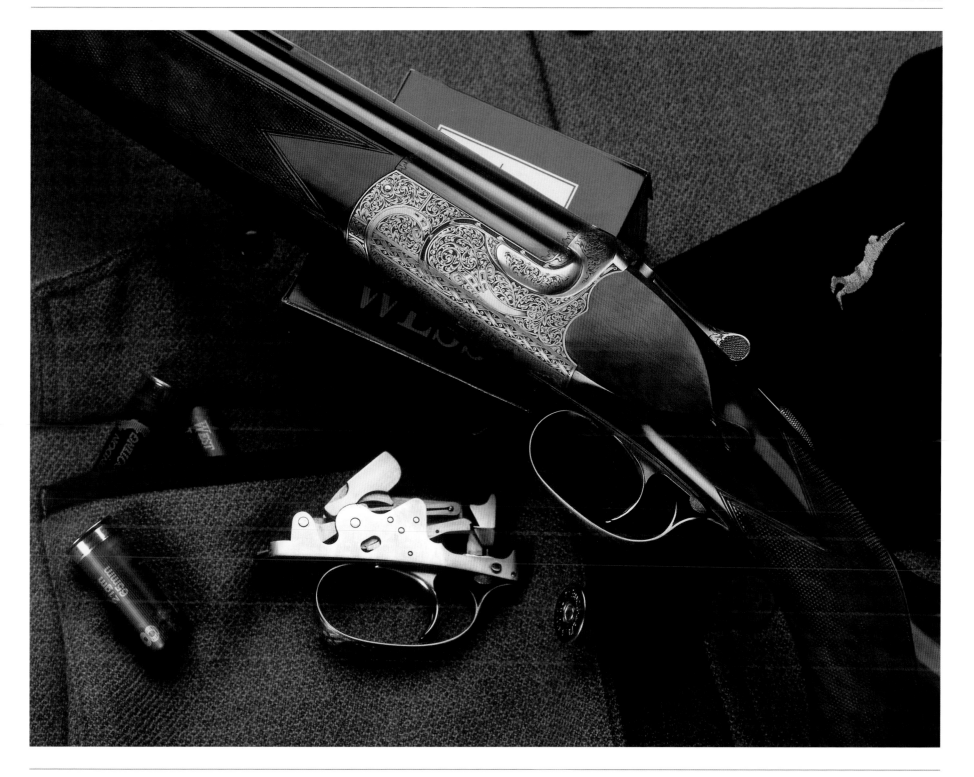

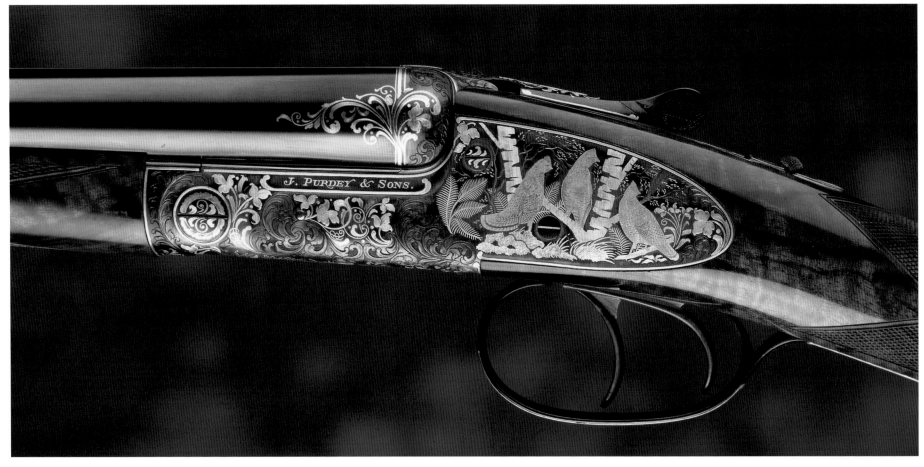

PLATE 102

James Purdey & Son 28-bore Ultra-Round Bar Sidelock

The first 28-bore sidelock built on Purdey's ultra-round bar action, this gun was
completed in 1998 for an American collector. It features Phil Coggan's
innovative multi-coloured inlays of America's ruffed grouse (pictured here)
and woodcock with coloured inlays of vegetation typical of their habitat.

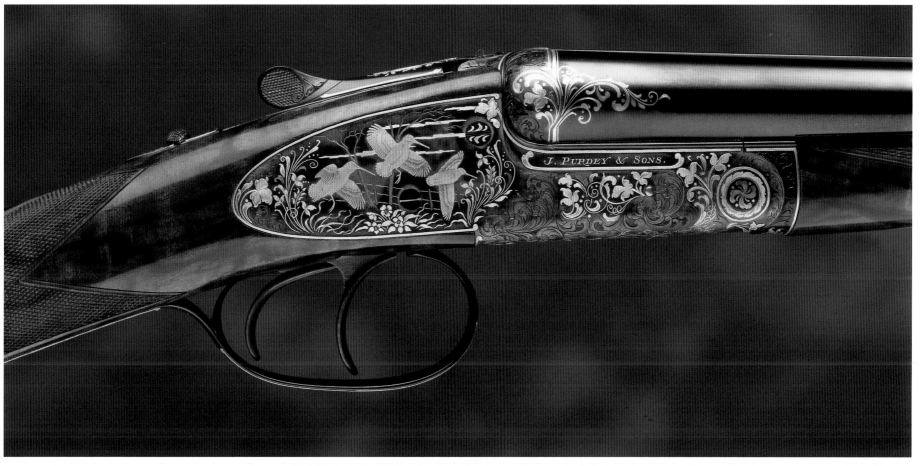

PLATE 103

James Purdey & Son 28-bore Ultra-Round Bar Sidelock

The right lockplate of Purdey 28-bore (Plate 102), with North American woodcock framed by flush inlays of multi-coloured gold foliage. The large scroll on the rounded bar is inset with multi-coloured flush and raised gold inlays.

PLATE 104 *(left)*

James Purdey & Sons 20-bore Round-Bodied Sidelock

Known as the 'Platinum Woodcock Gun', this Purdey 20-bore manages to be simultaneously opulent and understated. It was the first Purdey 20-bore to be built on a .410 action; with its slim rounded bar and a slender, cylindrical stock wrist, it was engraved by Alan and Paul Brown. The gun showcases flush gold scroll inlay, with the platinum inlays of woodcock raised and carved, all framed on dark case colours beautifully rendered by hardener Richard St Ledger. Note the acorn and oak leaf inlays on the fences (or 'detonators' in Purdey parlance) — aesthetically magnificent and also ecologically accurate to woodcock habitat. It was completed in 2000.

PLATE 105 *(right)*

James Purdey & Sons Miniature Hammergun

One of three miniature hammerguns made by Purdey's Harry Lawrence for the 1935 Silver Jubilee of King George V. A pair was presented to the King, while Purdey retained this one. Astonishingly each is a working gun, designed for firing tiny cartridges. When assembled each is seven inches long, and a testament to the skill of Purdey's gunmakers.

PLATE 106 *(left)*

James Purdey & Sons 20-bore Four-Barrel

The company's only known hammerless four-barrel, Purdey gun No. 11614 was finished in 1886 and built for a French colonel.

PLATE 107 *(right)*

James Purdey & Sons .577 Double Rifle

Completed in 1999, this Purdey .577 NE double rifle has deeply carved scroll and portraits by Alan and Paul Brown of Africa's 'Big Five'. Relative to its total production, Purdey has built relatively few hammerless double rifles.

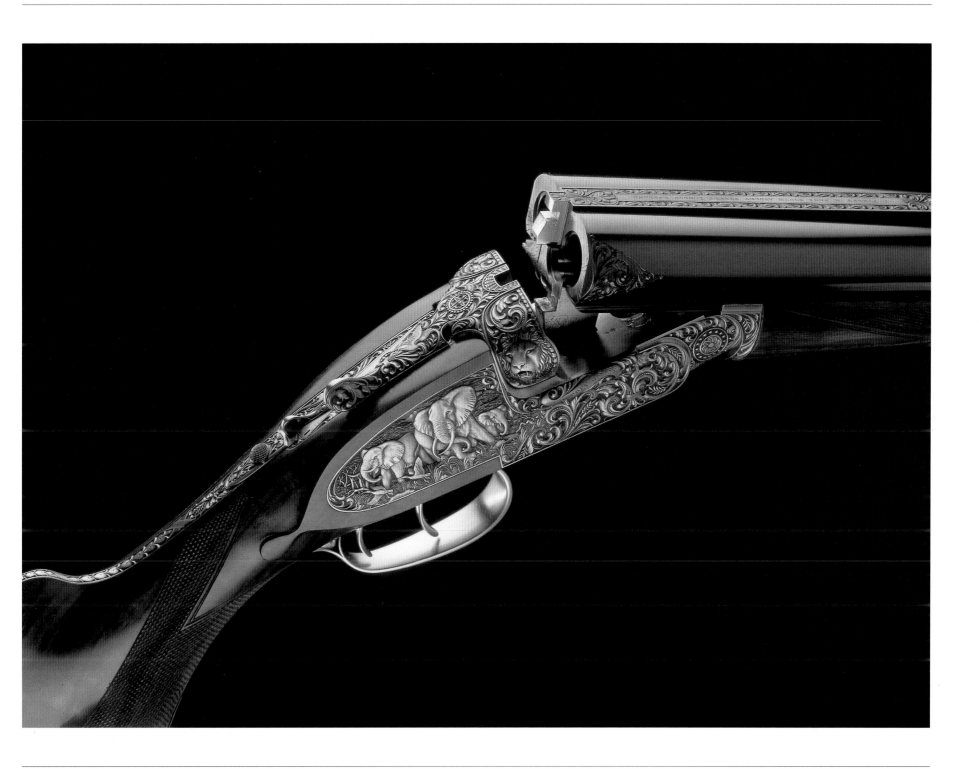

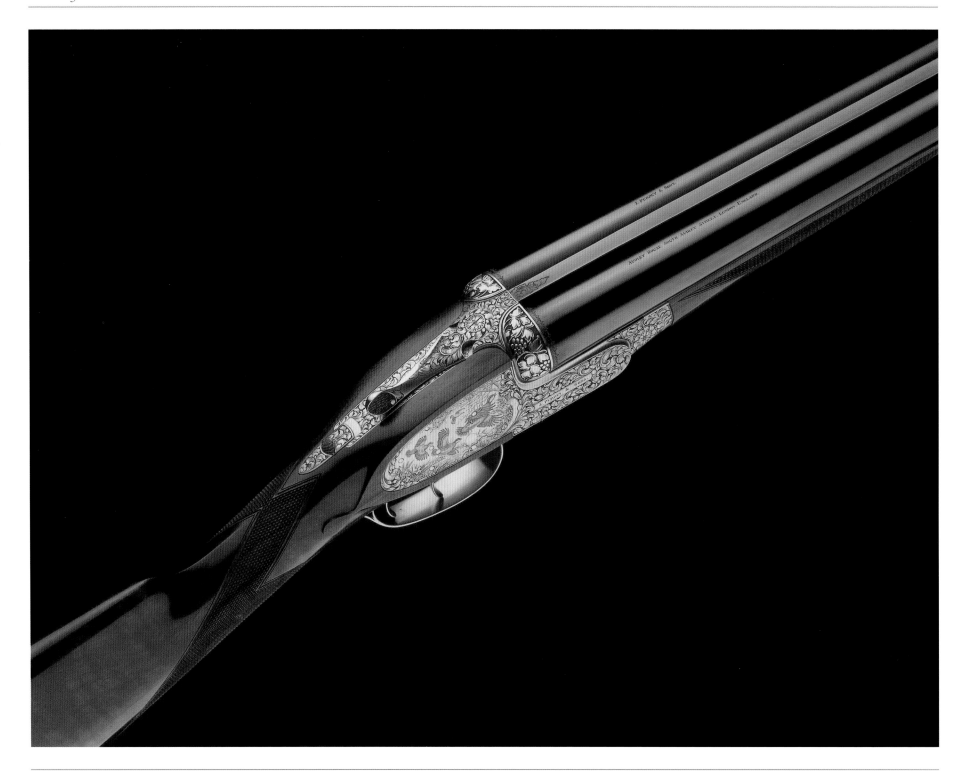

PLATE 108 *(left)*

James Purdey 12-bore Sidelock Side-by-Side

A recent Purdey self-opening 12-bore, built on the traditional 'square' bar action. It has large scroll engraving framing game-scene vignettes, with carved fences (or 'detonating'). All Purdey sidelocks are today built on dedicated action sizes, and are available in traditional square shape, round bar or ultra-round bar.

PLATE 109 *(right)*

James Purdey & Sons 28-bore Sidelock Over/Under and 20-bore Sidelock Side-by-Side

High Art Purdeys à la Alan and Paul Brown: The Platinum Woodcock Gun *(right)*, seen here with the 'Renaissance Guns', a 28-bore over/under with carved scenes from Classical Italian mythology. The background to the carving on the over/under is overlaid with gold. Though a far cry aesthetically from the chaste rose and scroll-engraved guns that helped make Purdey famous, these modern-day masterpieces capture the quality to which best British artisans are working today.

PLATE 110

James Purdey & Sons 12-bore Sidelocks

This pair of exhibition-grade sidelock Purdey 12-bores was completed in 2009. Each was engraved with scroll and gold by Nigel Westaway and weighs 6lbs 11^1/$_2$oz.

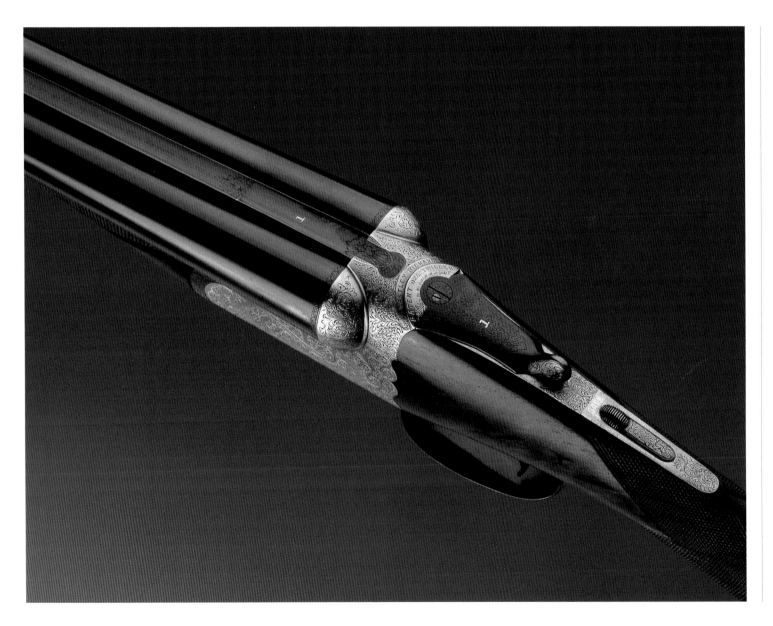

PLATE 111

Westley Richards 12-bore Hand-Detachable Lock Shotgun

In 1875 Westley Richards changed the course of world sporting gun history with the introduction of its Anson & Deeley boxlock – the world's first commercially successful hammerless gun cocked by the fall of the barrels. In 1897, Westley's changed history again with the introduction of its boxlock with hand-detachable locks – the 'droplock' in American parlance. This example, circa 1906, shows a Westley hand-detachable in full glory, with best fine scroll and the firm's single trigger. It is mechanically identical to the version Westley builds today, down to the company's distinctive – and effective – toplever and bolting system.

PLATE 112

Westley Richards .410 Hand-Detachable Lock Shotgun

This .410 hand-detachable, built in the late 1980s and engraved by Alan Brown, typifies the return of Westley Richards from near ruin in the decades following the Second World War to a best gunmaker capable of competing with London's finest marques. Only six .410 hand-detachables had been built historically, and the run of latter-day .410s – as evidenced here – were the result of company owner Simon Clode marrying his firm's modern engineering technology to traditional craftsmanship. The new .410s also marked the return of the hand-detachable lock to regular production, and it is once again offered as a rifle in a host of big-game calibres, as well as in 8-, 10-, 12-, 16-, 20-, 28-bores, and .410.

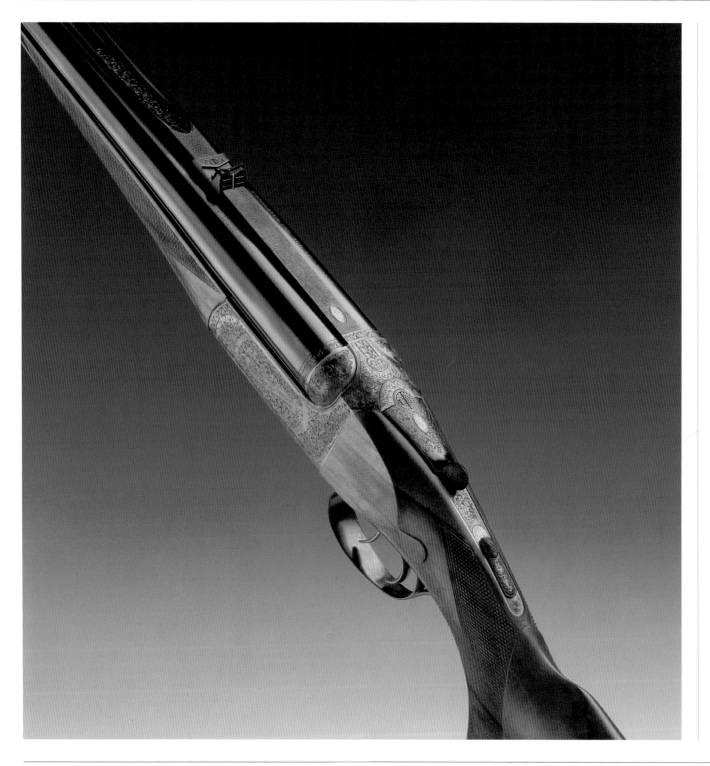

PLATE 113

Westley Richards .470 Hand-Detachable Lock Double Rifle

One of a pair of new .470s built to match a pair of .375s for the same client – a classic example of the Westley best-quality 'droplock' double rifle that has made the firm famous with big-game hunters worldwide for more than a century.

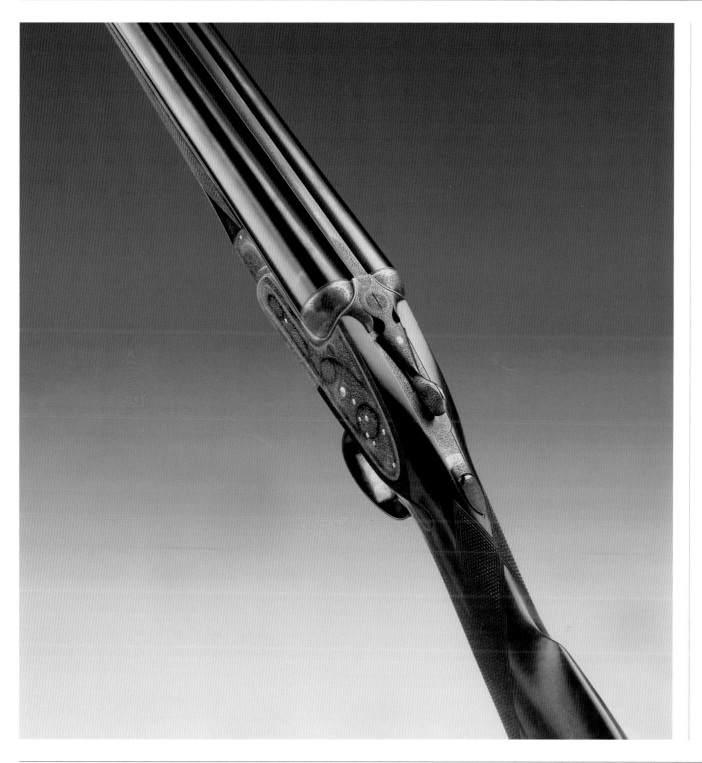

PLATE 114

Westley Richards 12-bore Sidelock

Though most famous for its Anson & Deeley actions, Westley Richards has long offered sidelocks. This bar-action example is a classic London-pattern gun, including the Purdey-style rose and scroll engraving. Its top safety, however, is more associated with Birmingham-made sidelocks.

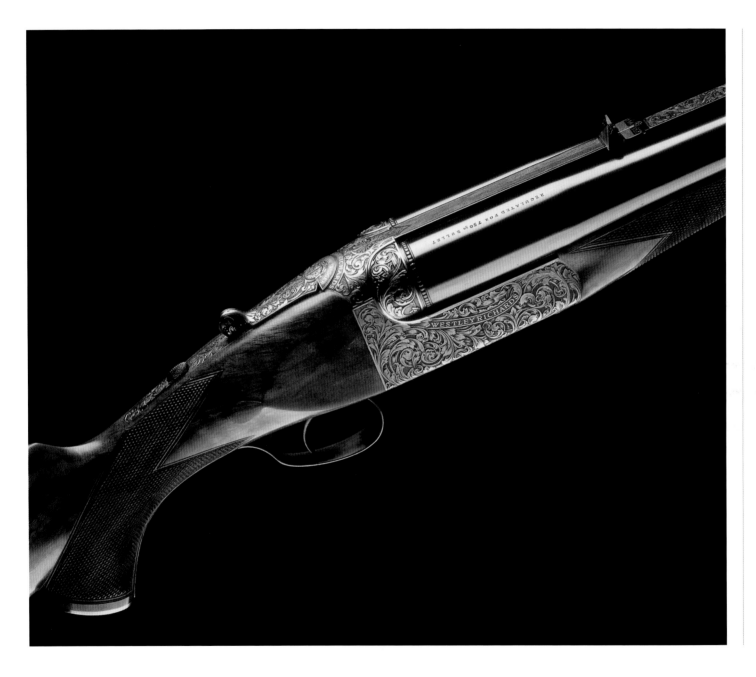

PLATE 115

Westley Richards .577 Hand-Detachable Lock Double Rifle

This new .577 hand-detachable is fitted with Westley's famed 'Patent One Trigger'. It weighs 13lb 8oz and has full coverage of lush foliate scroll by house engraver Vince Crowley. On average, over half of Westley's annual production currently consists of double- and bolt-action rifles, most in big-bore calibres.

PLATE 116

Westley Richards .458 Winchester 'Deluxe' Hand-Detachable Lock Double Rifle

This 'Deluxe' configuration of a recent hand-detachable lock double rifle in .458 Winchester is sideplated to provide a larger canvas for upgraded engraving – in this case Peter Spode's depiction of lions framed by cutaway scroll. The action has been semi-rounded and the stock lacks drop points, while arcaded fences are another atypical although elegant aesthetic addition to this big-bore Westley.

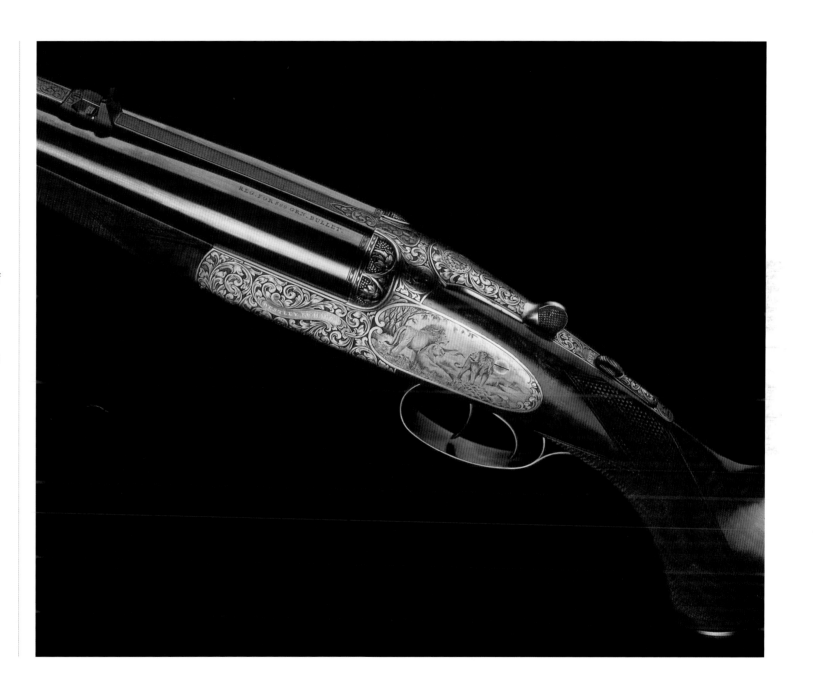

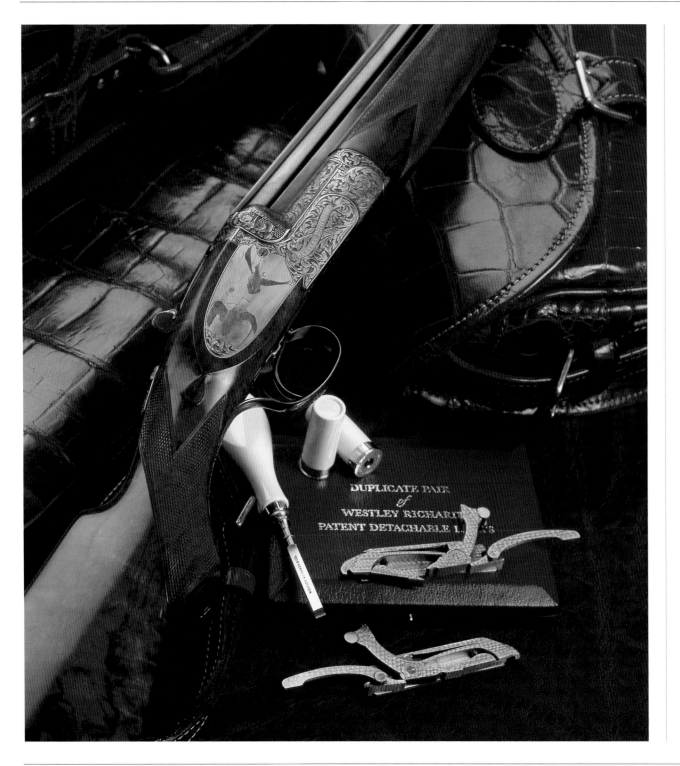

PLATE 117

Westley Richards 20-bore 'Ovundo' Over/Under Shotgun

A new sideplated 20-bore 'Ovundo' over and under with hand-detachable locks, and alligator-skin case and bags – all made in-house at the Westley factory. Allan Portsmouth engraved it with birds of prey and Westley's bold scroll. Continuing in the company's long tradition of building guns for much of the world's royalty – this example was one of a set of sixteen guns and rifles built for a prominent Middle Eastern family.

PLATE 118

Westley Richards 20-bore 'Ovundo' Over/Under

A close-up of the first 'Ovundo' to be built since the late 1930s, this new 20-bore remains faithful in design to its predecessors. The 'Ovundo' is unique in that it is all Westley Richards' design: in addition to its hand-detachable locks, its bolting system, toplever, top safety bolt, ejectors, hinged cover plate and selective 'Patent One Trigger' are all in-house inventions. As pictured here, it also showcases a patented hinged trap-door on the sideplates that allows access for lubricating the trigger mechanism. Though the Ovundo's action is visually less sleek than that of a Boss or Woodward, these are light guns that handle well – this one weighs 6lb 4oz.

PLATE 119

Westley Richards .300 Weatherby Magnum Mauser Take Down Bolt Action Rifle

A true left-handed double square bridge Mauser '98 action in .300 Weatherby Magnum, engraved by Shaun Banks with cut-back scroll and fine-line gold work. Birmingham's Richard St Ledger performed the colour-case-hardening.

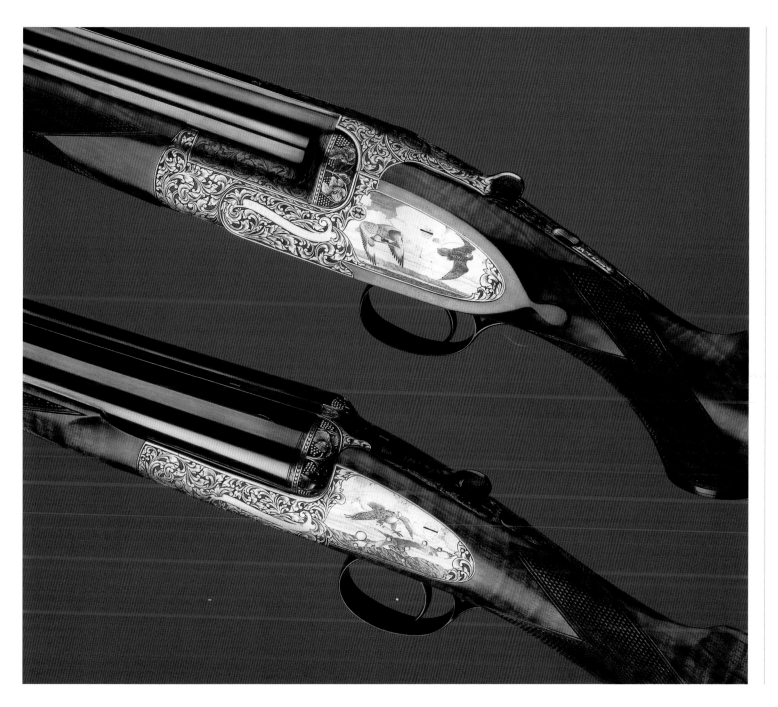

PLATE 120

Westley Richards 'Ovundo' and Round-Bodied Sidelock

The new 'Ovundo' and a new round-bodied sidelock side-by-side. WR's round-bodied sidelock was developed in 1997 and employs Boss-type locks, Holland-type easy opener, Southgate ejectors, and an improved inertia single trigger based on W.W. Greener's conceptual design. The action shape is reminiscent of a London Boss, but is more rounded throughout compared to the latter. Both guns are indicative of the diversity and quality of gunmaking available at Westley Richards in the twenty-first century.

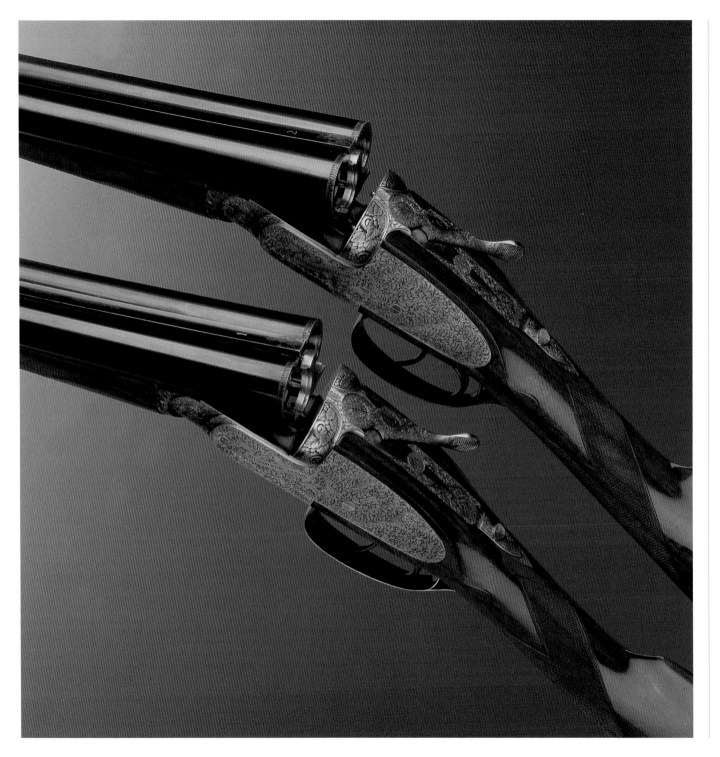

PLATE 121 *(left)*

David Sinnerton 20-bore Sidelocks

Purdey-trained gunmaker David H. Sinnerton completed this pair of 20-bore best sidelocks in 2004. Engraved in bold scroll by Wesley Tallett, they were built on Holland-type actions but showcase a number of Sinnerton's preferred stylistic signatures, including: Boss-style top strap (short with high shoulders) and disc-set strikers. Sinnerton is regarded as one of Britain's finest independent finishers to the trade, and has also built guns under his own name since 2001.

PLATE 122 *(right)*

David Sinnerton 28-bore Sidelock Over/Unders

Sinnerton completed this trio of Boss-style over/unders in 2007, the first Boss o/us under his own name. The guns took Sinnerton and his team of craftsmen about 1,800 hours and three years to complete and feature inertia-regulated triggers to the maker's design. They were embellished in Italy by engraving cooperative Creative Arts with game scenes of quail against a backdrop of lush foliate scroll. Triggers aside, they are otherwise built to the traditional Boss & Co. design.

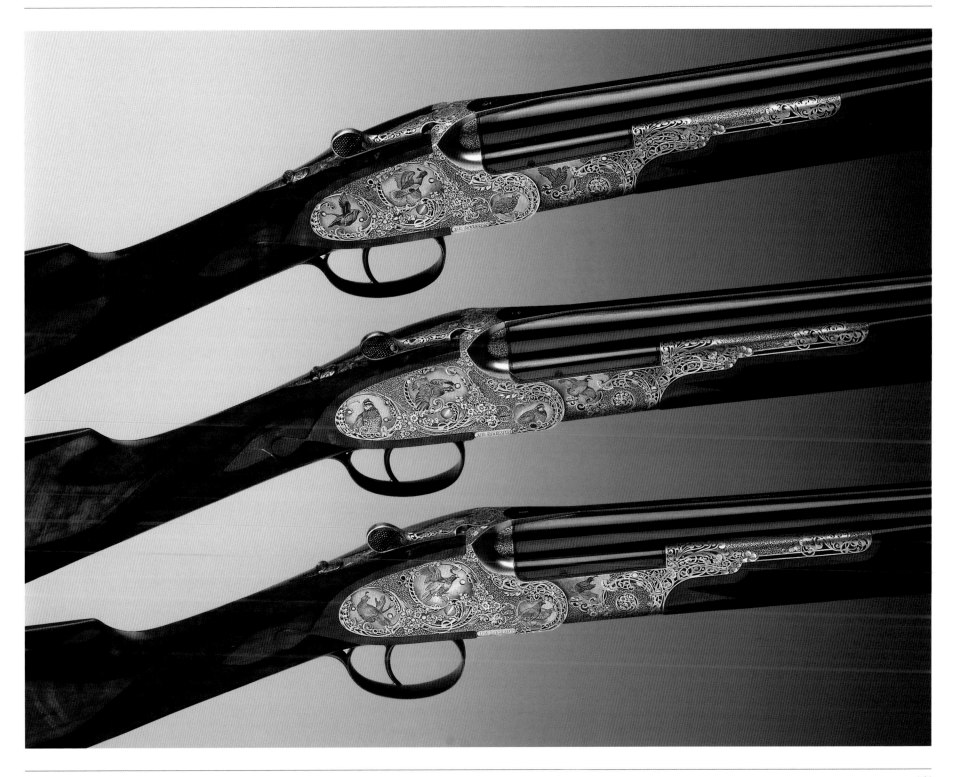

PLATE 123 *(left)*

C.H. Smith 12-bore Boxlock

Gordon Smith, then owner of Birmingham's C.H. Smith, made this lovely boxlock in 1988. Smith actioned the gun and made the furniture, then finished it. Barry King was the stocker and Roy Yeomans the barrelmaker. It is fitted with a single trigger and was engraved by Keith Thomas. The sculpting of the fences and action shoulders is particularly noteworthy – and the gun serves as a fine example of the high quality turned out by some of Birmingham's lesser-known makers.

PLATE 124 *(right)*

Turner Richards (Gunmakers) 12-bore Sidelock

Robert E. Turner, a respected gunmaker to the trade, recently completed this best-quality sidelock game gun – one of the few guns built under his own company moniker in his five decades on the bench. Bearing the Turner Richards (Gunmakers) name, it was built for a private customer and was made on an easy-opening Holland-type action and is custom-configured for a left-hander. It was stocked by Peter Rowland and engraved by John Barratt, a talented newcomer to the British engraving scene. Turner has spent virtually his entire career deliberately shunning publicity, but has built – and designed – guns for some of Britain's most famous retail names. When photographed, the gun was still in-the-white and had not been finished out.

PLATE 125

Watson Bros 12-bore Sidelock SxS Pigeon Gun and 12-bore Over/Under

In modern times, London's Watson Bros has become best known for its rounded-body
sidelocks, especially its over/unders. Lightweight 12-bore o/us – such as the Ken Hunt
engraved example pictured here – have become something of a house speciality.
Despite that, the firm – under the tutelage of Purdey-trained gunmaker Michael Louca –
builds a wide variety of bespoke London guns, from triple-barrel side-by-sides to 4-bore
double guns to traditional-frame pigeon guns to heavy o/us for high-pheasant shooting.
The side-by-side pigeon gun (pictured left of the o/u) was engraved by Keith Thomas
with game scenes, carved oak leaf fences and pierced toplever and triggerguard.

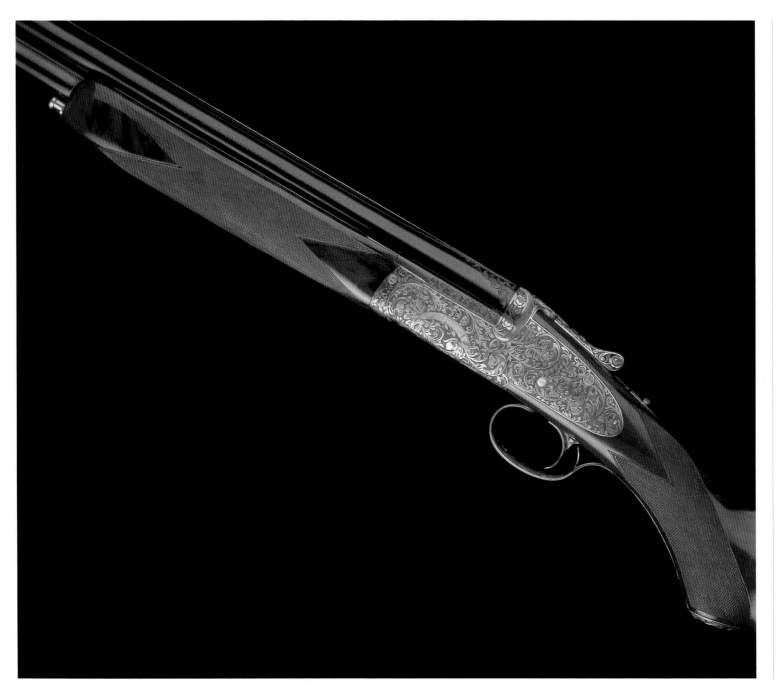

PLATE 126

Watson Bros. 20-bore Sidelock Over/Under

This 20-bore over/under has 30-inch barrels but weighs only 6lb. Watson's Michael Louca spent years developing a design to create lightweight o/us, with its centrepiece being new ejectorwork that permits both the forend and action to be reduced in size and made proportionately sleek. A variety of house engraving patterns come standard with each gun, and Watson's tend to be engraved in bold patterns, like Geoff Moore's foliate scroll on the gun pictured here.

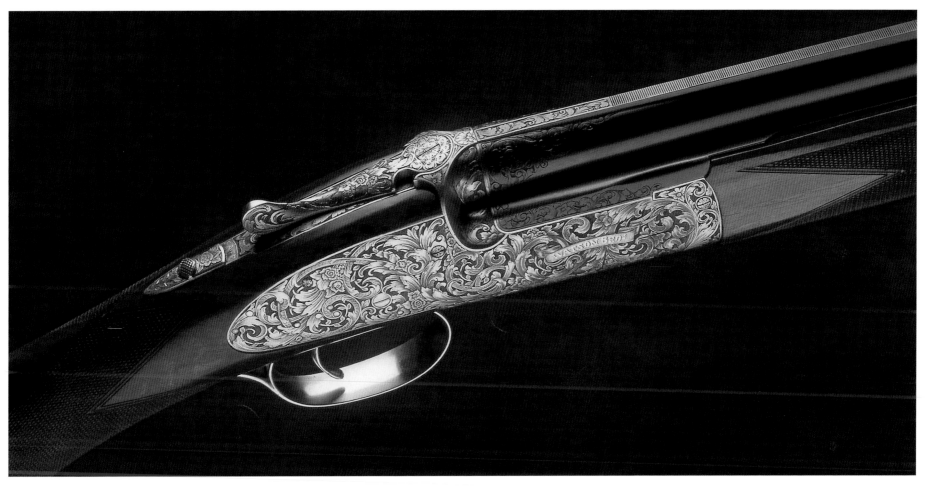

PLATE 127

Watson Bros 28-bore Sidelock Over/Under

With 29-inch barrels, this 28-bore weighs 5lb 12oz and showcases the lines of
Watson's rounded-body over/under. The distinctively shaped 'detonating'
(or fences) at the breech is a Watson Bros house style, as is the Edwardian
ornamental engraving pattern. Louca's goal from the outset has been to make
distinctive guns in-house to his own mechanical and aesthetic designs.

PLATE 128

Watson Bros 20-bore Sidelock Side-by-Side

After its relaunch in 1989, Watson Bros made its mark
first by producing rounded-body sidelocks on the
Beesley/Purdey self-opening action. Although the Boss
aesthetic provided initial inspiration, gunmaker Michael
Louca refined its stylistic signatures to his liking – sleek
lockplates and a short top strap leaves more wood in
the horns of the stock, permitting the lockplates and
grip to be made more cylindrical. The action is also filed
up with a coffin-shape taper, giving the gun a racy
profile. This 20-bore example weighs 5lb 15oz and was
engraved by Peter Cusack with his modern take on
fruiting vines and grapes with a game scene inset.

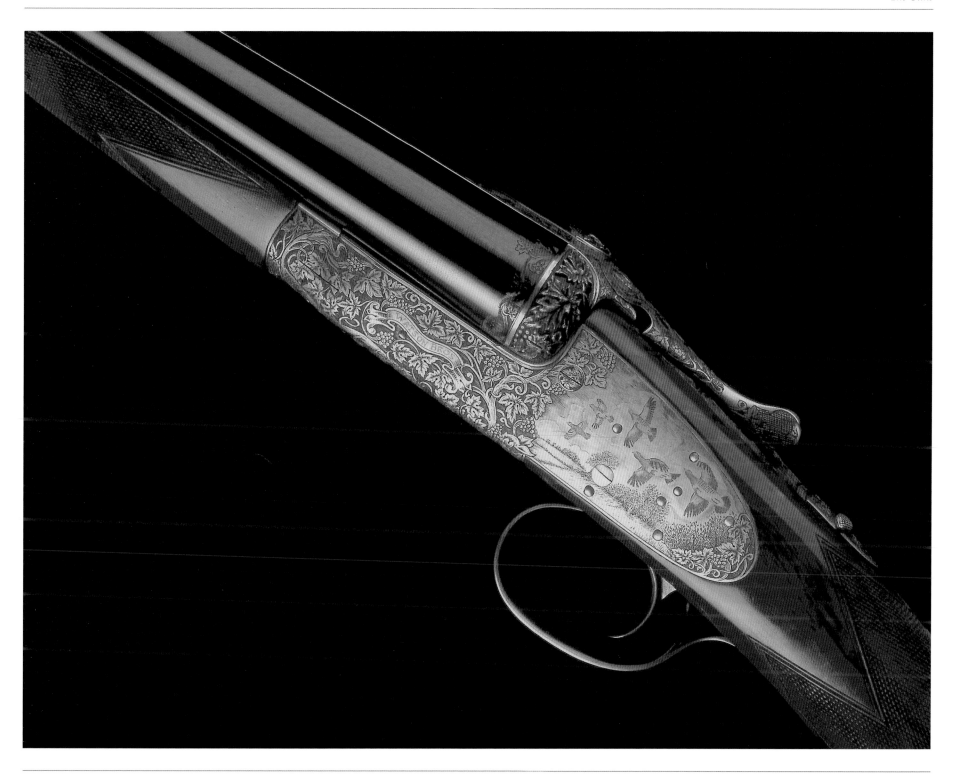

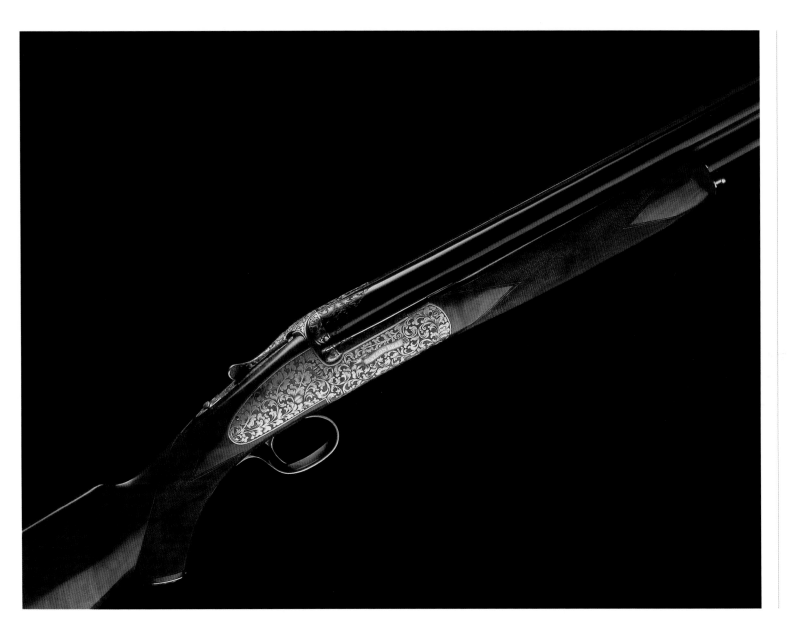

PLATE 129

Watson Bros 12-bore Sidelock Over/Under

This 12-bore with 30-inch barrels was made for a Canadian client and specifically designed for sustained high-volume shooting. At 7lb 3oz it has a heavier-than-typical action and the pins have been bolstered with locking pins to prevent them loosening under the vibration of heavy loads (a pin with locking pin is visible in lockplate behind lower barrel). This gun was engraved by Martin Smith.

PLATE 130

Watson Bros .375 Bolt Rifle

In its original incarnation, Watson Bros was, paradoxically, known for both its smallbores and its rifles, many of them big-bores. This .375 bolt rifle, with a 24-inch barrel, was made on Mauser 98 action and was engraved by John Barratt.

PLATE 131

Watson Bros .500 Double Rifle

Watson Bros made this .500 double rifle on a Holland-type action with Southgate ejectors. Made for a safari shooter, its fences and Holland-style bolster were carved by Keith Thomas, with the pinless lockplates engraved in foliate work by John Barratt. On average Watson makes about two rifles year.

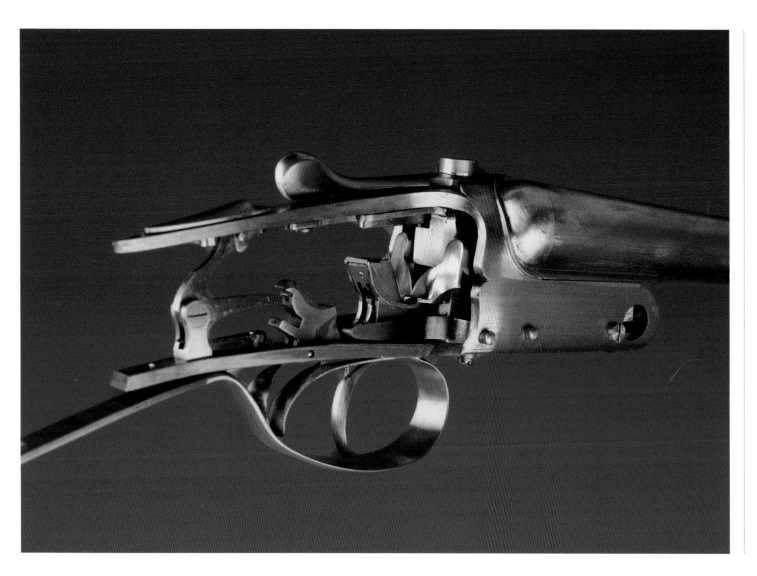

PLATE 132

T.R. White Boxlock Action in-the-white, with patented intercepting sears

Traditionally intercepting sears on a high-grade boxlock were hung on a pin that penetrates the shoulders of the action – an arrangement that can lead to heavier-than-desired trigger pulls. Tony White and actioner Ted Atkinson experimented with the concept and mounted White's version on the triggerplate instead. The interceptors are operated by a cam on the end of each trigger blade. When the trigger is pulled, the cam moves down, pulling the interceptor away from the tumbler and permitting it to fall.

PLATE 133

T.R. White & Co. Lightweight 12-bore Sidelocks

White and his team built these entirely British-made sidelocks in 2004 on Holland & Holland-type easy-opening actions with acanthus scroll and gamescene engraving by Peter Spode. With 29 inch barrels and 15³/₈-inch stocks, they tip the scales at 6½lb each – light for modern sidelocks with this barrel and stock length. The walnut came from White's personal cache of genuine French walnut and the game scene engraving was designed by Wales-based sporting artist Owen Williams. The latter was asked to incorporate four game-bird species into his artwork, and his did so with an eye to avoiding the pins protruding through the sidelock plates as much as possible. Spode added the lush scroll that frames the scenes and kept the engraving style as close as possible to the original artwork.

PLATE 134

T.R. White & Co. 20-bore Sidelock Over/Unders

These 20-bore rounded-body White sidelock over/unders
were completed in 2008. Actions were filed as round as
possible with vestigial bolsters left on the sides. With 29-inch
barrels and Prince of Wales grips each comes in at just under
seven pounds. Peter Spode executed the game scenes
framed by bold acanthus scroll. In 1996, White developed a
prototype rounded-body triggerplate over/under design, but
subsequently decided to pursue sidelock o/u models.

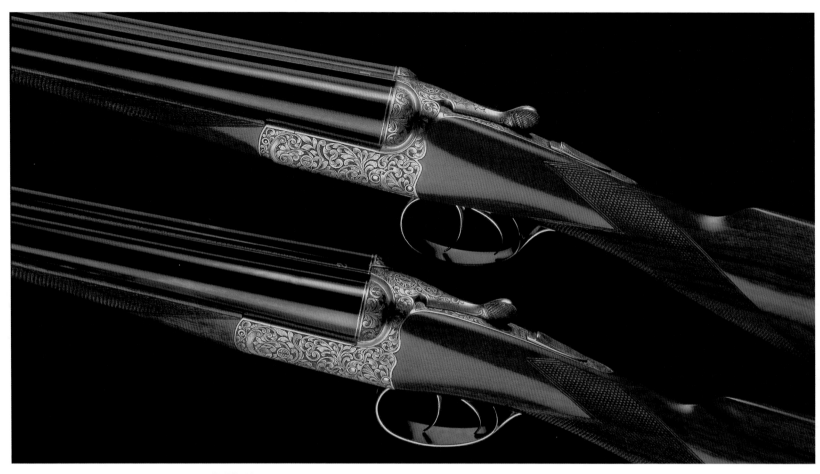

PLATE 135

Pair of T.R. White & Co 12-bore Rounded-Body Boxlocks

This pair of rounded-body boxlocks was made with White-patent intercepting sears and engraved by Geoff Moore. White achieves a rounded appearance with his boxlocks by elongating the curve at the shoulders of the action where it meets the top strap behind the fences, and by sculpting the back of the action down to the triggerplate to eliminate any straight lines. The action underside is also filed as round as possible. Other quality touches include chopper-lump barrels, rolled-edge triggerguards, rocker safeties, and removable hinge pins.

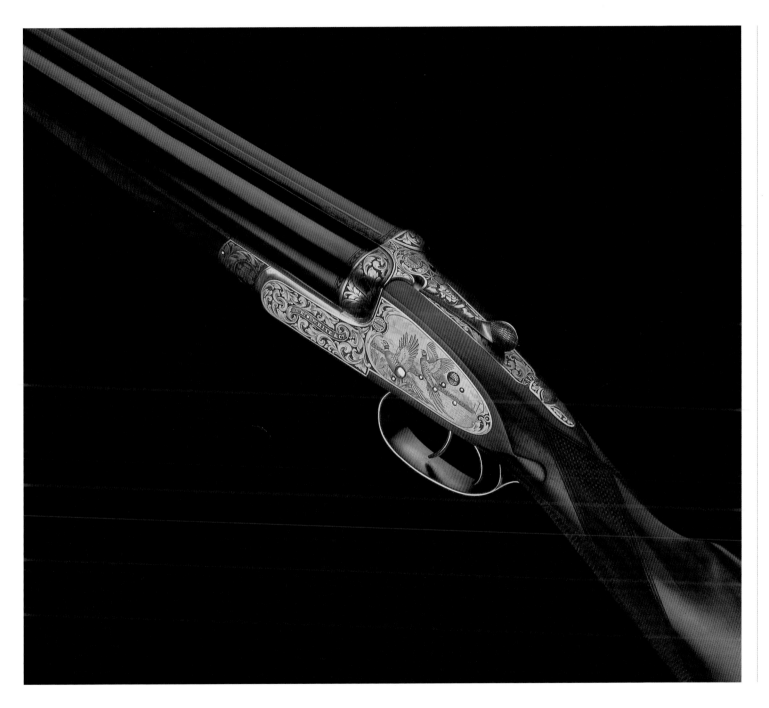

PLATE 136

T.R. White & Co. 12-bore Sidelock

Another Tony White Holland-type sidelock, also engraved by Peter Spode. Although Spode works almost exclusively as a house engraver for Westley Richards, he embellished this gun in his spare time – 'in the evenings, weekends and bank holidays' – as a favour to close friend White. It was commissioned by a client who shot in England and Scotland and both English roses and Scottish thistles were incorporated in the scroll. The client also provided photos of favourite locations where he shot, and requested these as backgrounds for the game scenes, which were to include pheasant and grouse. Said Spode: 'His gun reflected his shooting preferences and became a very personal item.'

PLATE 137

Best 20-bore William & Son Sidelocks

Officially a best gunmaker for only two years when this pair of William & Son 20-bores was completed in 2004, William Asprey's roots in London's best bespoke tradition date back to 1781, when an ancestor of the same name founded a firm that would later trade as 'Asprey'. William & Son was founded in 2002, after initially trading (from 1999 to '02) as 'William R. Asprey, Esq.'. These 20s are Holland-action guns, weighing 5lb 12oz each, and were engraved by Peter Cusack with deep foliate scroll in a pattern of his design.

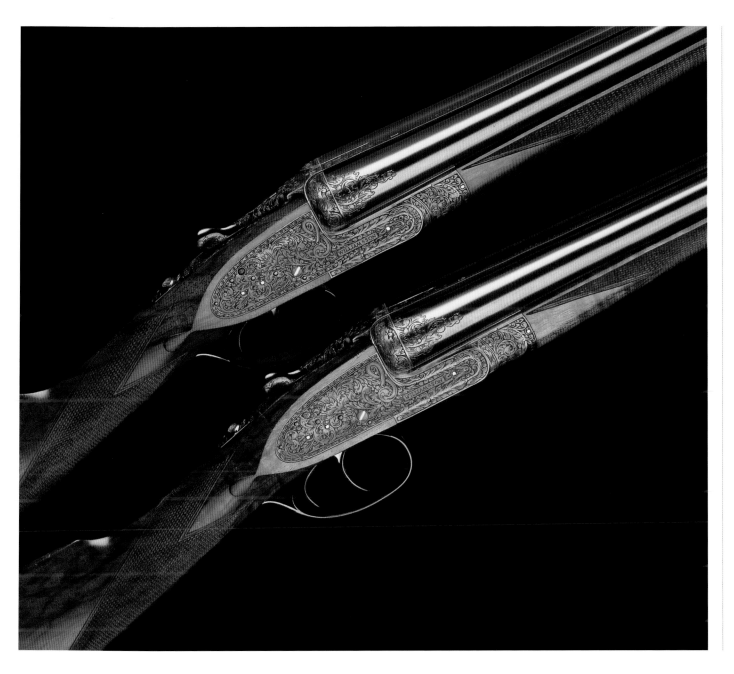

PLATE 138

Best 20-bore Colour-Hardened William & Son Sidelocks

A pair of colour-case-hardened William & Son 20-bores, completed in 2007 by actioner Mark Sullivan and his gunmaking team. Peter Cusack engraved these to William's house-scroll style, which was designed by Keith Thomas. Most William & Son guns are built on the Holland 'Royal' pattern, but the firm is now offering a new proprietary over/under.

PLATE 139

James Woodward & Sons 12-bore Over/Under and Side-by-Side

These Woodwards were made in the late 1990s, and were built in the factory of owner James Purdey & Sons. The over/under is built on a slightly modified Woodward action, which Purdey has used for all its over/unders since acquiring the former's business in 1948. Per historical Woodward practice, the side-by-side is built as a conventional-cocking, non-self-opener — this example on the Rogers-patent action (No. 397 of 1881), which distinguishes it mechanically from the Beesley self-opening action used for Purdey's side-by-sides.

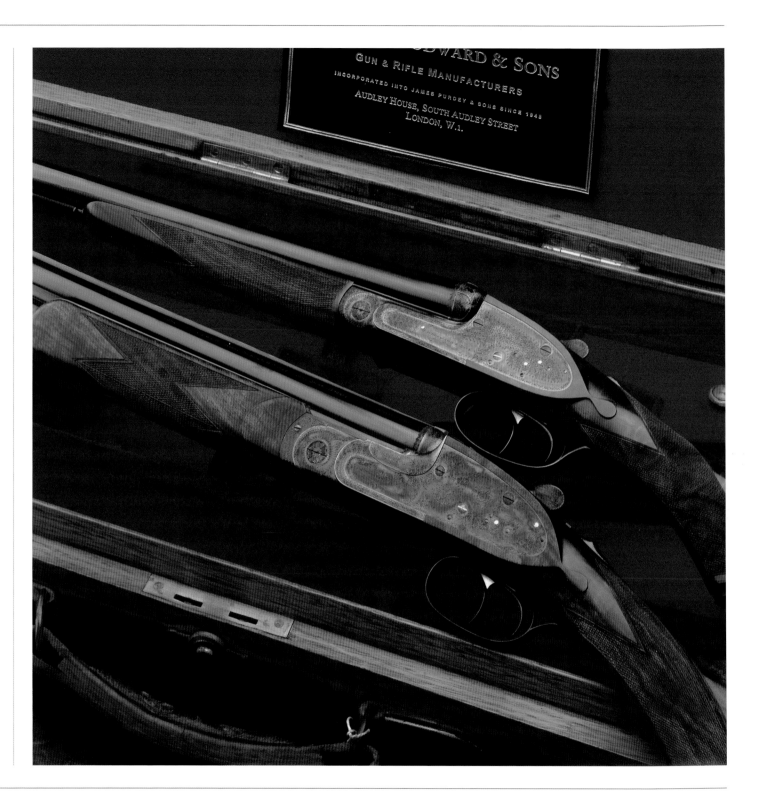

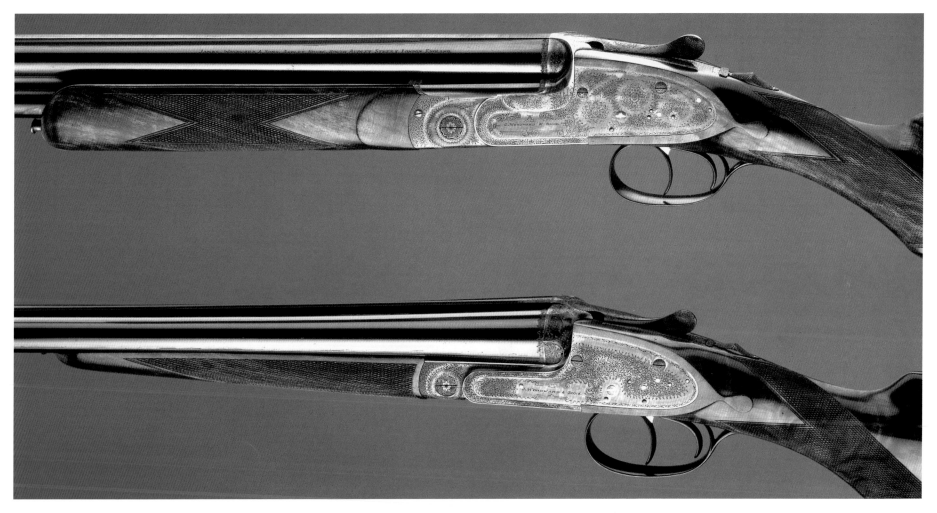

PLATE 140

James Woodward & Sons 12-bore Over/Under and Side-by-Side

Available again since 1997, new Woodwards replicate the aesthetics that helped
make them historically distinctive. True to Woodward style, the side-by-side has
its characteristic arcaded fences, a T-shape safety and tight scroll, with the
gunmaker's name on an engraved parchment banner. The over/under has the
firm's signature bolstered action shoulders, and both guns are stocked with
Woodward's trademark capped Prince of Wales semi-pistol-grip – or its
'Half-Hand Pistol Grip' in company parlance.

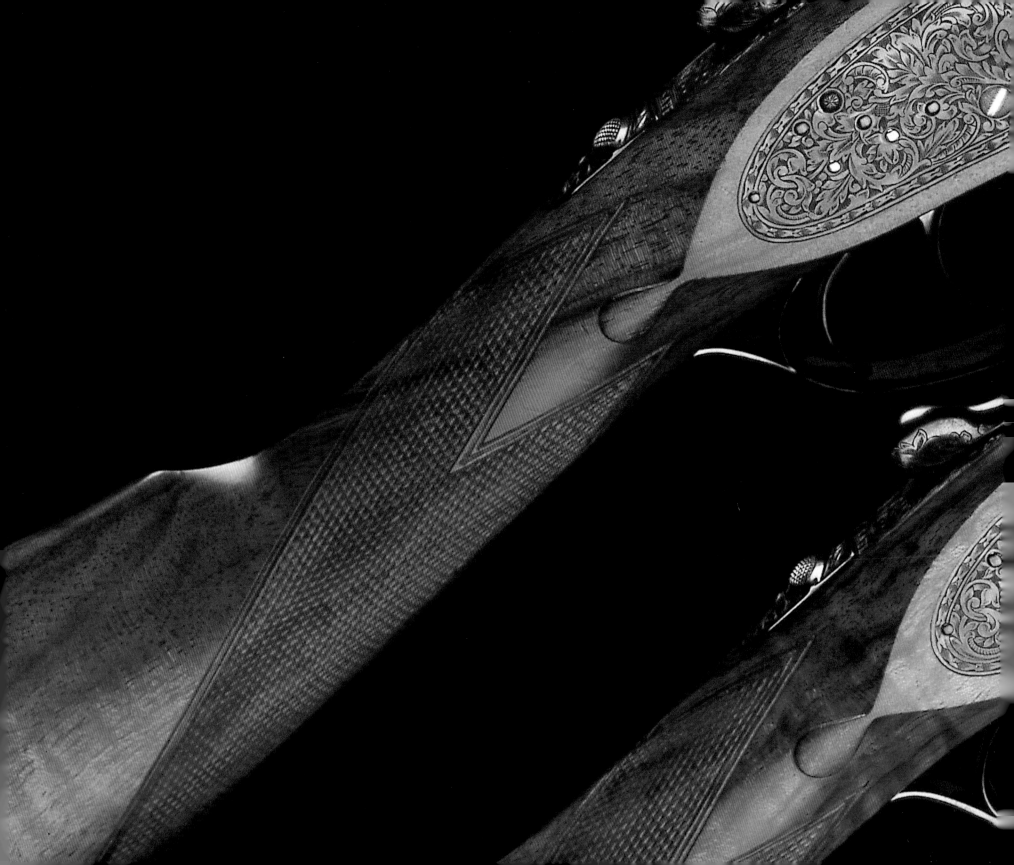

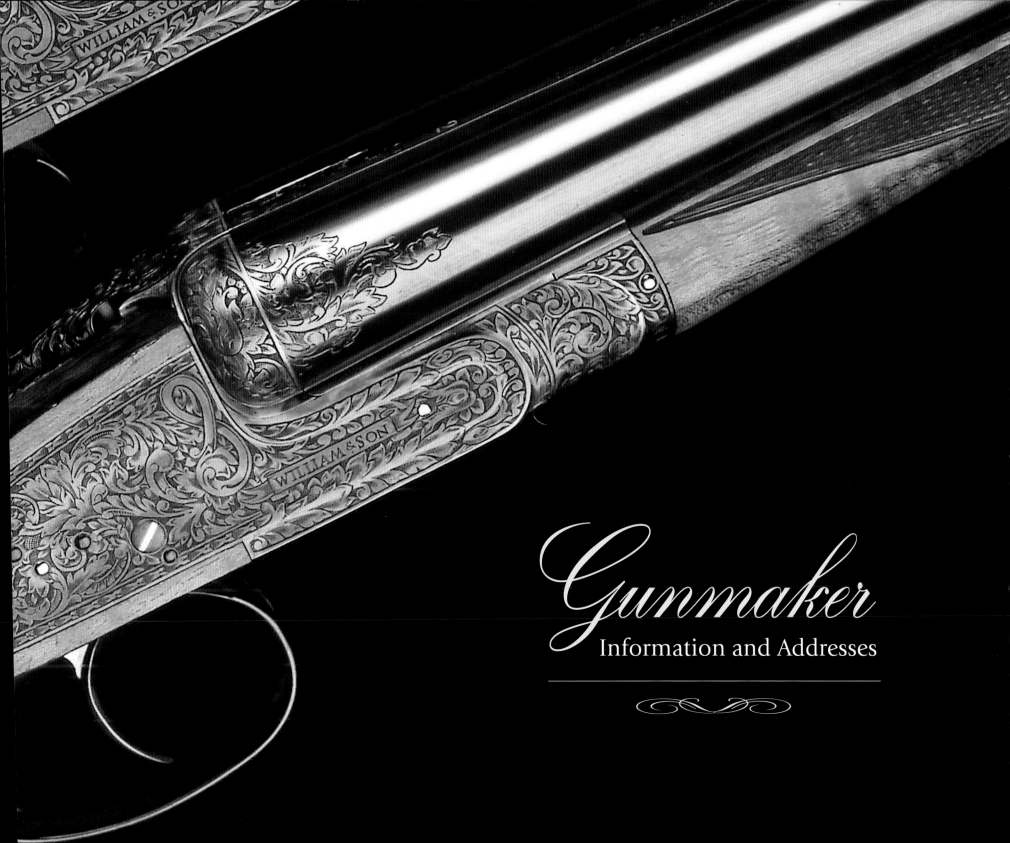

Gunmaker

Information and Addresses

Gunmaker Information and Addresses

Henry Atkin

Now part of the Atkin Grant & Lang gunmaking stable owned by Ken Duglan, Henry Atkin learned his trade in the mid-nineteenth century at James Purdey & Sons, having been apprenticed there to his father. In the mid-1870s he had become confident enough to open his own shop in London's Oxenden Street; by 1890 he was successful enough to move to a more prestigious address at 2 Jermyn Street. For a craftsman like Atkin to climb from the bench in class-conscious Victorian Britain to owning a shop patronised by aristocracy and the social elite was impressive. J.P. Morgan, Jr was only one of many prominent customers.

Observers at the time noted Atkin's ability to not only work to the highest standards himself but also to perceive those standards in the work of others – an invaluable talent when overseeing a team of craftsmen responsible for building best guns. Atkin made and marketed a wide variety of guns and rifles – but is today best known for the modified Beesley/Purdey-action self-openers introduced to the firm's line in 1907. These were built with modified Southgate-type ejectors, which allowed the guns to close somewhat more easily than those sold at the time by Purdey.

Atkin died in 1907, but the firm carried on under the directorship of family members and, later, the Hodges family of gunmakers. Its reputation served it well in coming decades, and Atkin survived the Depression, the Second World War, and the lean years following. By the late fifties, however, orders had fallen to the point that amalgamation with another maker was the best hope going forward, and in 1960 it merged with Stephen Grant & Joseph Lang to become Atkin Grant & Lang Ltd.

After the amalgamation, guns continued to be built under each of the respective names. In 1971, Churchill joined the group. The company moved to 61 Pall Mall in 1976 and remained there until 1980. The Harris and Sheldon conglomerate owned the firm briefly until 1984, when Cyril Adams, of Texas, purchased Atkin Grant & Lang. In 1997, Adams sold the company to Ken Duglan, owner of Broomhills Shooting Grounds, north of London. Duglan was a former Atkin employee who had worked at the firm under Alan Lawrie, the gunroom manager. Since that time, Atkin Grant & Lang has specialised in the restoration of best-quality guns built by the original firms; new guns are also made under each respective marque. Duglan has three craftsmen working in-house at Broomhills – finishers Alan Bower and Carl Russell, and apprentice Ian Sweetman – and he uses the skills of ex-Holland & Holland outworkers such as stocker Stephane Dupille, barrelmaker Bill Blacker, actioner Gary Hibbert, and finisher Alan Wey. An Atkin built today will typically be made on the firm's modified Beesley/Purdey action.

For more information, contact
Atkin Grant & Lang Ltd,
c/o Ken Duglan, Broomhill Leys, Windmill Road, Markyate, St Albans, Herts., AL3 8LP, England
01582 849382
info@atkingrantandlang.co.uk
www.atkingrantandlang.co.uk

Boss & Co.

Bigger isn't always better – and there is no better example in British gunmaking than Boss & Co. Though the smallest of London's 'Holy Trinity' in terms of production, Boss gives nothing away by way of intrinsic quality of craftsmanship or its legacy. In operation continuously since the early 1800s, Boss is perhaps best known for its transcendent over/under of 1909 – a design that not only underpins the mechanical principles of most of the world's great over/unders today but also still sets aesthetic standards yet to be bettered.

Boss's single trigger, ejectors, lock design, and aesthetics remain in use not only with the company but have also been widely imitated, or remain influential with other gunmakers.

Company founder Thomas Boss was apprenticed to his gunmaker father, William Boss, in 1804 – the latter at the time working for Joseph Manton. After completing his apprenticeship in 1812, Thomas

remained with Manton until 1816, when he set up as an independent gunmaker. From the outset, Boss only produced one quality of gun, and this policy has continued through to the present with the firm billing itself as 'builders of best guns only'.

Success followed and after several relocations, Boss moved in 1839 to 73 St James's Street, an address from which the firm confirmed its reputation as one of London's premier makers. Thomas Boss died in 1857, with company reins managed by widow Emma and managing partner Stephen Grant (who in 1867 established his own business at 67a St James's.) The firm, by then trading as Boss & Co., continued under nephews Edward and James Paddison, who together proved competent-if-cautious gunmakers. The firm might have ended up remembered as just one of any number of superb nineteenth century London gunmakers had it not been for the arrival in 1891 of a new owner, the Scottish-born craftsman John Robertson. The reputation Boss enjoys today was cemented by Robertson's inventive talents. First came the Boss single trigger of 1894 – the first truly successful single trigger ever made – followed by 'spiral spring' driven ejectors of 1897. Robertson at the same time was also redefining best-gun aesthetics with its rounded-action sidelocks and distinctive rose and scroll, the latter engraved by the Sumner family. Both remain hallmarks of the firm. It was Boss's sidelock over/under, however, that assured the firm's immortality in gunmaking history. By fitting the hinge, bifurcated lumps and bolting system along the lower barrel, Robertson and Boss craftsman Bob Henderson obviated the need for under-lumps, which previously had necessitated deep, often graceless actions on Continental competitors. Not only did Boss launch a revolution in mechanical design but also another aesthetic one: there is hardly a best-quality over/under built anywhere in the world today that does not in some way pay homage to either Boss's elegant, stepped forend iron or the action's shell-like, recessed fences.

The great designs – and the immaculate finishing the firm was known for – helped Boss & Co. soldier on under Robertson family ownership through two world wars, depressions and recessions. By the late 1970s, however, it was trading as much on reputation and repair work as contemporary gunmaking. The great double-gun revival of the 1980s helped a turnaround begin: by the mid-eighties the Boss over/under was again being made in 12-bore after a production hiatus of two or more decades. By 1992 20-bore versions and side-by-side double rifles were under way.

In December 1999, the Robertson family sold Boss & Co. to an investment group headed by Kenneth Finken, who appointed new management and moved shop (and factory craftsmen) to Mayfair's 16 Mount Street.

In early 2001, Boss changed hands again, this time being sold to the Halsey family, with Graham Halsey named Managing Director. The Halseys have made substantial financial investments to return Boss to its former glory. A 3,000-square-foot factory was purchased near Kew Gardens, in Richmond, and new machinery and production facilities moved there. Currently ten full-time craftsmen work at the benches, with a maximum annual production of twenty guns (up substantially from that of the 1990s). Side-by-side and over/under guns and rifles are still made entirely to original Boss designs, and largely by traditional craft techniques. Nowadays about sixty-five per cent of new orders are for over/unders, and in 2010 o/us will once again be built in 28-bore and .410, with a 16-bore o/u planned for 2012.

The Boss single trigger – 115 years old and still going – is today requested for most over/unders and for about fifty per cent of new side-by-sides. In 2008, Boss's lease on Mount Street expired and the firm moved all operations to its factory at Kew, although a return to Mayfair is planned for 2010 for retail operations.

For more information, contact
Graham Halsey, Boss & Co. Ltd,
Kew, Richmond, Surrey (Visits by appointment only)
020 7493 1127; fax 020 8605 3684
info@bossguns.com

Charles Boswell

Charles Boswell was born in 1850 in modest circumstances and by hard work and his talent in the pigeon rings made a reputation for building guns for competitive live-bird shooters in Britain and abroad – especially in Australia and South Africa. He founded his business in 1869 in Edmonton but by 1884 had moved to 126 The Strand, in central London. A trade label of the era notes Boswell was 'Winner of 40 Cups Open to All England'. Many of Boswell's guns were high-quality boxlocks of pigeon-gun configuration, often elaborately embellished – and regardless of design those built for professional shooters were invariably well made. In 1914 Boswell's son, Osborne George assumed management and in 1922 the firm moved to South Moulton Street. In 1924 Charles Boswell died and in 1932 the Boswell firm was on the move again, this time to 15 Mill Street. Here they were bombed-out by the Luftwaffe in April 1941. Osborne George passed away months later and his widow continued the business until 1944 – after which point the family connection apparently ends.

After several post-Second World War overseas ownerships – the last being Florida's Garfield R. Beckstead – the brand was revived in 2004 by British shooting instructor Chris J. Batha, who along with Beckstead is an owner. At time of this writing (spring, 2009) Batha has delivered thirteen new guns and rifles and has nineteen others in production, with a speciality in smallbores – or 'Baby Boswells' as Batha calls them. Some of the over/unders have been built on Italian-sourced actions (*FAMARS di Abbiatico & Salvinelli*), while others are of British origin and are built to the Woodward/Purdey type. Side-by-sides are also of English origin, either Holland-type easy openers or Beesley/Purdey-type self-openers. Batha uses British outworkers – among them finisher David Sinnerton, gunmaker Mark Sullivan, barrelmaker Mick Kelly and stockers Bobby Smith and Andy Marshall – to finish out new bespoke Boswells.

For more information, contact
Chris Batha, 43 Pinckney Colony Rd., Okatie, SC 29909-4100
Chrisbatha@aol.com
www.chrisbatha.com

A.A. Brown & Sons

Not Britain' largest gunmaker, nor its oldest, nor its most famous, A.A. Brown & Sons nonetheless accomplished what no other Birmingham firm was able to do in the latter half of the twentieth century. During the post-Second World War era, when virtually all Birmingham firms were either declining in size or simply shutting down, A.A. Brown by contrast was growing. Moreover the quality of its guns was such that during the 1970s they were able to make a transition from being an anonymous 'gunmaker's gunmaker' to becoming a highly respected maker for retail clients. Though Brown is smaller now than in its heyday, its signature gun – the Supreme De Luxe – is still judged as one of England's finest easy-opening sidelocks, and director Robin Brown enjoys the same respect from his peers on the bench that his grandfather, Albert Arthur Brown, once enjoyed.

The latter, an actioner to the trade, founded his business in Birmingham's gun quarter in 1929. In 1938 Albert Arthur was joined by sons Albert Henry (1913 to 2001) and Sidney Charles (1916 to 2006), and from that time on the firm was known as A.A Brown & Sons. Much of their work during the Depression era was for makers such as E.J. Churchill. During the war, Brown was involved in defence-related contract work and its Sand Street premises were bombed. It was during the lean years in the 1950s that Brown exhibited an ability to prosper and expand, even as others in Birmingham trade were contracting and moving into repair work. During this period the firm purchased the machinery of trade maker A.E. Bayliss and that of action-machinist Joseph Asbury, thereby bringing virtually all the manufacturing aspects of gun production in-house. Lockmaking and colour-case-hardening were later added to Brown's in-house capabilities. Although many better-known gun factories across Britain were struggling to find, train and keep craftsmen, Brown by contrast had a full team of seasoned artisans working its benches, most of whom had begun their careers before the Second World War.

By the late fifties, the firm was building a wide variety of guns for the London, Birmingham and provincial trade, from modest A&D boxlock 'poverty guns' for Cogswell & Harrison to best sidelocks for the likes of E.J. Churchill and Holland & Holland. In 1960, the company moved to Westley Richards's factory complex, where they continued to work for the trade at large, as well as to build Westley's sidelocks. They also developed and made the latter's 'Connaught' model Anson & Deeley boxlock. During this time, Brown's employed nine full-time craftsmen, and was building some 200 to 250 guns per year. Robin Brown (born 1946 in Birmingham), grandson of the founder and son of Sidney Charles, joined the firm as an apprentice in 1961, training first as a stocker but also as a colour-case-hardener.

In 1974 Brown left Westley Richards to establish a stand-alone factory of its own in Alvechurch, a village south of Birmingham. The move was more than geographic: it marked the end of Brown's days as a trade maker and the beginning of its ascent as a producer of best-quality sidelocks for retail customers.

With the deaths of his uncle and father in 2001 and 2006, respectively, Robin Brown is now sole proprietor. Brown's continues to make the Supreme De Luxe, as well as perform renovation and restoration work. As much work as possible remains in-house – performed by completely traditional craft methods – though Robin also employs the services of London-trained barrelmakers and stockers to supplement his skills.

For more information, contact
Robin Brown, A.A. Brown & Sons, One Snake Lane, Alvechurch,
Birmingham, B48 7NT, England
0121 445 5395
www.doubleguns.co.uk

David McKay Brown (Gunmakers) Ltd

It has never been easy to establish a reputation from scratch as an independent gunmaker; it is harder still to take a world-famous gun design and make it your own. David McKay Brown has accomplished both.

Since 1974, the Glasgow-based maker has built guns under his own name based on the Scottish Round Action. In so doing, Dickson's celebrated design from the 1880s has become for many – particularly in the United States – the 'McKay Brown Round Action'. With his evolution of the design to an over/under variant, the identification of Scotland's greatest gun with McKay Brown is almost complete.

McKay Brown, born in 1941 in the mining town of Bellshill, began his gunmaking career in 1958 when he signed on as an apprentice with Alexander Martin Ltd, in Glasgow. When Dickson purchased Martin in the early 1960s, McKay Brown trained part time at the former's premises in Edinburgh, where he learned the principles of making the firm's famed Round Action and completed his apprenticeship. At the time, in-house gunmaking was almost gone at Dickson and McKay Brown set up independently in March 1967, in Hamilton, near Glasgow. Though he continued to work for his former employer, his dream was to build Round Action guns under his own name. In 1974, after four years of tooling up and development, McKay Brown completed the first Round Action bearing his name.

The Round Action has always been a design unto itself, with little

gunmaking precedent in London or Birmingham, so McKay Brown had to train his own workforce of specialists to build them. These include Brian Moir, actioner; Brian Sinclair, stocker; Douglas Proctor, stocker; and Jim McDonald, barrelmaker. Together they have over a century's experience served at McKay Brown.

In 1980 a burgeoning order book prompted a move to bigger premises in Bothwell, by Glasgow. During the eighties McKay Brown began considering an over/under, based on the Round Action's triggerplate principles. Development took about a decade but in 1992 McKay Brown registered the design and a year later his Round Action over/under was launched to great success. Today, it forms about seventy per cent of recent production, which amounts to about thirty guns per year.

Guns to both configurations are available in 12-bore through .410, with the smallbores being offered on proportioned actions. Rifles are available in side-by-side configuration, in a variety of big-bore calibres. Although guns are built in Scotland in McKay Brown's workshops, about eighty per cent are engraved in Italy, many by noted engraving cooperative Creative Art, which offers high quality with timely turnaround at reasonable prices.

For more information, contact
David McKay Brown, 32 Hamilton Road, Bothwell, Glasgow G71 8NA
01698 853727; Fax:01698 854207
info@mckaybrown.com
www.mckaybrown.com

E.J. Churchill

The enduring prestige of a select few gunmakers – Purdey's, being a prime example – may lead some to believe that gunmaker reputations are immutable through time. This is only rarely true.

The case of Churchill provides a classic example of how the favour and fortune of a gunmaker can rise and fall and rise again with almost cyclic regularity, depending on a host of factors both internal and external to the company in question – and also by the force of personality of its management.

Founder Edwin John Churchill was apprenticed at William Jeffery, of Dorchester, before moving to London to work for F.T. Baker. He established in own business on Agar Street in 1891, and made his reputation building pigeon guns. A crack shot, he was also a superb gunfitter and his guns were popular among the professional shooting fraternity. Churchill's fortunes began to decline as pigeon shooting fell from popularity in England in the early twentieth century, and he spiralled into depression upon the death of his son, H. E. J. Churchill, in 1902. Nephew Robert raised capital and rescued the firm after Edwin's death in 1910, and guided Churchill through the difficult war years (incorporating it as E.J. Churchill (Gunmakers) Ltd, in 1917).

In the years before the First World War, Robert Churchill, aided by general manager Jim Chewter, began experimenting with short-barrelled guns, culminating in the early twenties with the brilliantly promoted 'XXV' concept. Churchill declared longer barrels obsolete, and the fast-handling guns built by him around 25-inch barrels were a genuine improvement on the past and the key to improved shooting. His claims and resulting controversy with traditionalists sent publicity – and sales – soaring. By 1925, demand for XXVs outpaced the firm's ability to build them. Envious gunmakers throughout the twenties and thirties increasingly attempted to emulate Churchill's success with their own shorter-barrelled, lighter-weight guns – though none became quite so synonymous with a maker as did Churchill's XXV.

Today XXVs and other short-barrelled guns are roundly out of favour with shooters on both sides of the Atlantic, and some latter-day observers have attributed Churchill's success with them to marketing genius alone. In fact, XXVs were effective – so long as a shooter was properly schooled in the techniques (or 'drill', in Churchill's words) developed to shoot light, low-inertia guns, and when ranges were kept to less-than-long distances. Churchill's popular shooting-instruction books *How to Shoot* and *Game Shooting* were no doubt instrumental in creating cadres of converts to his style. Churchill's guns – or Churchill-style guns – remained popular with a substantial minority of shooters even after his death in 1958.

In 1959 the firm was purchased and the name changed to Churchill (Gunmakers) Ltd and in 1964 the latter acquired Atkin Grant & Lang. In 1971, the companies were amalgamated with the creation of Churchill, Atkin Grant & Lang Ltd. By then the firm was suffering from crippling inflation and the spiralling costs associated with bespoke British gunmaking, as well as the generalised economic malaise of much of the decade. In 1980, Churchill ceased operation, with its remaining stock of new guns auctioned off in 1981 in Dallas, Texas.

Don Masters, Churchill's former production manager, registered the name E.J. Churchill (Gunmakers) Ltd in 1984. In 1996, West Wycombe Shooting Grounds Ltd obtained rights to the Churchill Gunmakers Ltd name and began efforts to revive it. After a disputatious beginning, the two parties were able to come to agreement, allowing West Wycombe to begin resuscitating the Churchill brand.

For more information, contact

E.J. Churchill Group Ltd, Head Office: Park Lane, Lane End,

High Wycombe, Bucks HP14 3NS

01494 883227

www.ejchurchill.com

George Coster & Son

George Coster was the son of George Ernest Julius (Julius) Coster, a German-born gunmaker who left his homeland to work with Edinburgh's Alex Henry in 1869. Julius was the son of German gunmaker Johann Cristoph Koster – and the late Geoffrey Boothroyd speculates Julius may have brought to Scotland the genesis for the McNaughton 'Edinburgh' and Dickson Round Actions due to similarities with Germany's 'Blitz' triggerplate designs. The truth is likely lost to time, but regardless both Julius and son George were talented gunmakers working in the Scottish tradition of impeccable workmanship. After rising to the equivalent of works manager for Alex Henry, Julius formed a partnership with a Mr Hunter in 1886, trading as Coster & Hunter in Edinburgh until 1890, when the business dissolved. Julius continued to work independently until the late 1890s, when he moved shop to Glasgow and worked for Charles Ingram. Around 1920, father and son worked together as George Coster & Son, of 145 W. Nile Street. Julius died in 1927 and George, trained as a stocker, carrying on the business until 1930, and then going to work for Alex Martin, where he stayed until retirement. According to Boothroyd, one of his sons (also George) worked for Martin and a daughter married another gunmaker employed by Glasgow's Arthur Allan. In 1993 the Coster name was obtained by Glasgow Gunmakers Ltd (now trading as Graham Mackinlay & Co. Gunmakers). Mackinlay indicates that no records have survived, and the Coster name is currently inactive as a gunmaker.

For more information, contact

Graham Mackinlay, Strathleven House, Dumbarton Glasgow G82 3PD

01389 751122

enquiries@gmackinlay.com

John Dickson & Son Ltd

Few names encapsulate a culture's gunmaking tradition quite so thoroughly as Edinburgh's John Dickson & Son. Not only is it responsible for perfecting and popularising the signature gun of Scotland – the Round Action – but Dickson also gobbled up many of its worthy Caledonian competitors, thus preserving gunmaking traditions that would have otherwise likely been lost.

The original John Dickson was born in 1794 and he was apprenticed to Edinburgh gunmaker James Wallace in the early nineteenth century. By 1840 he was trading as a gunmaker under his own name at 60 Princes Street, moving nine years later to the old Wallace premises at 63 Princes, where the firm traded until 1929.

By the late 1850s Dickson's was dabbling in then-new breechloaders, but it was in 1880 that the firm really came into its own with Patent No. 294 – the patent progenitor of the design that was to become the Dickson Round Action. It would take three more patents – No. 873 of 1882 and Nos. 9393 and 10621 of 1887 – for the gun to fully evolve. The 1882 patent also provided for three-barrel versions, which were made in small numbers in a variety of configurations. Notably Dickson also produced some side-opening over/unders – similar in principle to Belgium's Superbritte. The 1880s through the First World War were the firm's halcyon years. The last Dickson to manage the business died in 1923, although the firm was run by successors energetically enough to begin purchasing competitors: Mortimer and Harkom in 1938, MacNaughton in 1947, Martin and Henry in the sixties. The firm has since changed ownership several times, most notably in 1999 when the owners of James MacNaughton (who had purchased the latter from Dickson in 1995) in turn purchased the shareholding of Dickson and renamed the firm Dickson & MacNaughton. Dickson's Edinburgh premises at 21 Frederick Street – occupied by the firm since 1937 – were extensively renovated and efforts initiated to revive gunmaking of the Dickson and the MacNaughton Round Actions, as well as expand new-gun offerings under the banners of its incorporated Scottish makers, such as Alex Martin, Alex Henry, Thomas Mortimer and Dan'l Fraser.

For more information, contact

John Dickson & Son Ltd, 21 Frederick Street, Edinburgh, EH2 2NE

0131 225 4218; fax 0131 225 3658
info@john-dickson.com
www.john-dickson.com

David J. Dryhurst & Richard Tandy

Geoffrey Boothroyd once described a young David J. Dryhurst as a 'new boy' in the Birmingham trade – 'one of the very few with the courage or temerity to break into a highly specialised field, for the Master Gunmaker, unlike the Independent Craftsman, has to sign his work and he has to be responsible not only for what he has done but also for the work of others who have helped create a "best" gun.' That was decades ago. No longer a 'new boy', Dryhurst, now sixty-seven, is today recognised as one of England's finest living gunmakers, not only for having built best guns for London's very best names but also for helping revive W.W. Greener Ltd and restoring its lustre as a best-quality British gunmaker.

Dryhurst was born in Rednal, on the outskirts of Birmingham, in 1943. He joined W.W. Greener in 1958 as an apprentice actioner – one of the last apprentices taken on by Greener before it was sold off in the mid-sixties. After short stints at Webley & Scott and Westley Richards, Dryhurst set up in 1965 in Birmingham's Price Street as an independent gunmaker 'because no factories were then building guns to the quality I wanted to make them'. An unstinting perfectionist from the start, he began building guns under his own name, and soon developed a core of retail customers.

In 1968, Dryhurst was approached by Holland & Holland for employment on an outworker basis and until 1987 he made sidelocks – Badmintons, Dominions and Royals – for the London firm. During this time, he also made sidelocks for William Powell, William Evans and Churchill, Atkin Grant & Lang Ltd. During the late 1980s and early nineties Dryhurst and fellow gunmaker Richard Tandy also made actions and best sidelocks *in toto* for Boss & Co.

Dryhurst had met Tandy in the early 1970s when the latter approached him for assistance in breaking into the gun trade. Dryhurst recognised Tandy's latent talent and convinced Don Masters, at Churchill, to hire him. Tandy, born in 1955 in Stourbridge, trained at Churchill as an actioner until 1976, before leaving to set up on his own. W.W. Greener had been revived in 1985, and Dryhurst invited Tandy to join the stable. By the mid-nineties, orders were sufficient for Dryhurst to be able to wrap up orders for the trade to concentrate only on new Greener production. Today Dryhurst and Tandy – assisted by barrelmaker Peter Higgins and stocker Peter Rowland – turn out Greeners to the highest standards of traditional best British craftsmanship.

For more information, *see*
W.W. Greener entry.

William Evans Ltd

William Evans may never have been a bench-trained gunmaker but he unquestionably had talent for selling their wares. The firm of the same name appeared in London in 1883 on 95a Buckingham Palace Road, with Evans having cut his teeth in the trade at both James Purdey & Sons and Holland & Holland. Information on Evans the founder is scanty: he apparently worked in sales at both businesses. He marked his early guns with 'William Evans (From Purdey's)' a promotional tactic that did nothing to endear him to his former employer. Purdey considered but then declined to take legal action. After all, James Purdey the Elder had done the same when he left Manton's employ earlier in the century. The controversy did nothing to hurt Evans, as business proved brisk enough to allow a series of moves to better premises, with the firm changing location four times in its first thirteen years of business. In 1896 Evans was able to settle at 63 Pall Mall, where it remained until bombed out during the Second World War. From Pall Mall, Evans was able to cultivate as clients officers posted to nearby Guards Regiments; early ledger books, in fact, are filled with the names of captains and colonels from Britain's military elite. The firm offered a wide variety of guns and rifles, from utilitarian to best grade. Many were made – or at least actioned – in Birmingham by P. Webley & Sons or W. & C. Scott, and after their merger by Webley & Scott. Its very best-grade guns were often made in the shops of top London outworkers, such as E.C. Hodges or John Robertson. Second-hand guns were a speciality, as were repairs, and also general outfitting for officers about to be posted abroad. After suffering extensive bomb damage in February 1944, Evans moved to 67a St James's Street, where it remains today. The company survived the post-war years that felled so many other gunmakers, and in 1991 it was reinvigorated when purchased by a consortium of private investors. Today the business has expanded into two buildings on St James's, and relies on much the same recipe that brought it success initially – new best guns built to order by top London craftsmen, and a friendly, accessible gun room (now headed by Alastair Phillips) that offers a good selection of second-hand guns of a variety of makes and models.

Clothing, accoutrements and accessories for the shooting lifestyle remain an important part of the business.

For more information, contact

William Evans Ltd, 67a St James's Street, London, SW1A 1PH

0207 493 0415

www.williamevans.com

George Gibbs

George Gibbs began making guns in Bristol around 1830 at 4 Redcliffe Street. Several moves followed in the mid-nineteenth century until the firm settled down on Corn Street from 1858 to 1890. Gibbs built a separate factory in 1873, and during the Victorian and Edwardian eras became famous for its rifles. These were popular with big-game hunters of the day, and the .505 Gibbs cartridge became widely known. In 1874, the maker patented the Gibbs & Pitt gun – sometimes dubbed the first commercially successful hammerless shotgun – a triggerplate design that cocked via its underlever (later a toplever-cocking variant was also produced). It was popular during the era in which many other transitional hammerless designs were vying for favour with the shooting public. By 1906 Gibbs's reputation had reached the point where it could open a London branch at 35 Savile Row. George C. Gibbs, the firm's founder, died in 1918 and company ownership passed out of family hands to a partnership. It went bankrupt in 1929 but survived in smaller quarters off Baldwin Street, in Bristol, after closing its factory and London premises. In 1964 Gibbs was purchased by Bath gunmaker I.M. Crudgington and Norman Harper. In 2007 I.M. Crudgington's son – stocker Mark Crudgington – purchased the name and continues making Gibbs guns.

For more information, contact

Mark Crudgington, The Granary, Brimslade, Marlborough, Wiltshire, England, SN8 4NG

011672 811765

George.gibbsltd@btinternet.com

www.gibbsgunmakers.com

Stephen Grant & Sons

American author Robert S. Braden was once quoted, 'God shoots an English hammergun.' The maker of said gun was not mentioned but Braden probably meant one made by Stephen Grant. Born a grocer's son in 1821 in Tipperary, Ireland, Stephen Grant had become by the time of his death in 1898 one of London's most respected gunmakers.

Young Grant served his apprenticeship with Dublin's William Kavanagh before moving to London in 1843 to work with Charles

Lancaster. In 1850, Grant moved to Thomas Boss and when the latter died in 1857 his widow made Grant a managing partner in the business. In 1867, Grant decided to work for himself, taking pains in 1871 to publicly disassociate himself with Boss. That same year he was appointed gunmaker to the Prince of Wales and over the next quarter century, he would establish the Grant name as one of the finest in London. Grant and his two sons were simultaneously clever inventors and were also quick to adopt promising patents by other talents.

Today Grant remains best known for its elegant and beautifully made sidelever sidelocks with distinctive fluted fences. Despite many designs to which Grant guns were built, the sidelever sidelock remains the signature gun of the company. When the elder Grant passed away, his widow and sons continued the business but by the early twenties deaths in the family and associated tragedies meant the business had to be sold. In 1923 it was purchased by William Robson, a Scotsman who amalgamated it with Joseph Lang & Sons in 1925.

Under Robson's tutelage, Grant & Lang went on to absorb many of its competitors during the Depression: Harrison & Hussey, Charles Lancaster, Watson Bros and Frederick Beesley. Post-war, the firm went on to join with Henry Atkin Ltd in 1960 and became Churchill, Atkin Grant & Lang Ltd in 1971. It appeared the great Grant guns were gone for good when the firm ceased trading in 1980, but Cyril Adams, of Houston, Texas, purchased Atkin Grant & Lang in the mid-eighties and revived best-quality gunmaking. In 1999, Ken Duglan, ex-Atkin Grant & Lang sales associate, purchased the trio of names and moved it to Broomhill Shooting Grounds, north of London. Duglan's craftsmen and outworkers continue to build both Grant sidelock side-by-sides and over/unders to classic British designs, and have made a speciality of restoring vintage Grant guns to as-new condition.

For more information, contact

Ken Duglan, Atkin Grant & Lang, Broomhill Leys, Windmill Road, Markyate, St Albans, Hertfordshire,.AL3 8LP

01582 84938; fax: 01582 842318

info@atkingrantandlang.co.uk
www.atkingrantandlang.co.uk

Edwinson C. Green

Several years ago gunmaker Peter V. Nelson was at The Vintage Cup – a sort of American mini-Gamefair that celebrates side-by-side double guns – where he was observed going from dealer's booth to booth, studying their wares, which included best guns from some of the world's most prestigious makers. When asked what was the finest gun he had seen be unhesitatingly pointed to a beautifully finished older sidelock. It bore the name: E.C. Green, Cheltenham. 'That's the best gun at the show,' he said. Coming from a perfectionist of his repute, Nelson's observation was high praise indeed.

Edwinson Charles Green was born in 1842 and trained in Birmingham, and was ambitious and talented enough to try making guns under his own name. Instead of heading to London, where most craftsmen of similar ambition went, Green chose the spa town of Cheltenham, where he opened a shop in 1867. Green and his family firm not only made guns to very high standards, but were innovators as well. His two most important designs were patent 15307 of 9 July 1902 – his three-barrel design (Plate 43) – and his over/under patents, 8225 and 14951, of 1912. Until Purdey purchased Woodward to obtain the latter's over/under, the former based its over/under on Green's design. In 1911, a Green-patent triple-barrel 16-bore took the gold medal at the Turin exhibition held that year. Nigel Brown's research indicates gunmaking ceased in 1947, though the firm remained in business through the late 1970s before closing.

W.W. Greener Ltd

No English gunmaker today has come full circle more completely than that of Birmingham's W.W. Greener. Arguably the most idiosyncratic of all Britain's famous makers, it has in the last decade and a half reestablished its reputation by creating contemporary gunmaking masterpieces that incorporate Greener's historic aesthetic and mechanical attributes.

William Greener was born in 1806 and originally hailed from the Newcastle area. After completing an apprenticeship, Greener went to work with London's Joseph Manton, remaining with him until 1829, when he returned north to begin gunmaking in Newcastle. Greener, ever ambitious, moved south to Birmingham in 1844, where the quality of his work earned him success in England and abroad. His books – *The Gun, The Science of Gunnery,* and *Gunnery* – were well known in their day, and remain classics on the muzzleloading era.

Son William Wellington followed in his father's footsteps in the business but the two split acrimoniously in the mid-1850s when the younger Greener began advocating newfangled breechloading guns. When the elder Greener died in 1869, W.W. amalgamated his father's business into his own, and – until at least the First World War – became one of Britain's biggest and most prestigious gunmakers. Greener's cross bolt and side safety were enormously influential (and remain staples of Teutonic gunmaking), as was his popularising of (if not inventing) choke boring. The operating principles of Greener's inertia/bobweight single-trigger design of 1898 have been widely copied. The firm's famed Facile Princeps action was the basis for the first commercially successful hammerless ejector – and was made in a variety of configurations and grades, many as elaborately embellished show guns. Though not as widely known today as London's Jack Sumner or Harry Kell, Greeners's house engravers – Messrs Tomlinson, Stokes, Horrocks and Gilmore – were arguably the Victorian era's best, or at least its most versatile.

Greener made vast numbers of guns from 1880 to the First World War – at least 60,000 of them 'hand-made' – but the war had a disastrous effect on the firm's export markets. Greener's business declined and the Second World War hastened its downturn. Post-war redevelopment of inner-city Birmingham, including its gun quarter, delivered the final blow, and Greener's factory was torn down and its name and assets sold off in the early 1960s. In 1985, a partnership – including Graham Greener (the great great great grandson of W. W. Greener), Ken Richardson and gunmaker David Dryhurst–purchased the dormant name and restarted gun production. Richard Tandy, a highly regarded actioner and single-trigger specialist, soon joined the trio to give Greener the in-house talents to reestablish itself as a best-quality gunmaker. Initially new Greener guns were mostly built as Holland-action, London-pattern sidelocks but by the mid-nineties Dryhurst and Tandy had attracted the attention of some of the world's most prominent collectors, and with those commissions in hand they were able to once again begin building exhibition-quality guns with many of the Greener features that helped make the firm famous a century earlier. For example, the proprietary G-Grade hammerless ejector (or 'G-Gun'), was returned to production in both smallbore shotgun and big-bore rifle variants. Several century-old G-Gun actions in-the-white, along with an unfinished best hammergun action, were also finished out and engraved by Alan and Paul Brown (see Plates 46, 47, 48 and 51). Greener's was the last British gun factory to forge its own damascus tubes and in the late 1990s it became the first maker in the world to return damascus-barrelled guns to regular production, using a cache of vintage tubes Dryhurst had collected since the 1960s. More than twenty-five 'new' damascus guns have been built or are currently under production. Today the firm concentrates on making exhibition-quality sidelocks with Greener features such as its proprietary-patent three-teardrop, five-pin bridle lockwork, hand-carved arcaded fences, and embellished with updated versions of its historic 'house' engraving patterns. Engravers include Alan and Paul Brown, Phil and Simon Coggan, Brad Tallet and Keith Thomas.

For new gun inquiries, contact
David Dryhurst
tigdry@yahoo.co.uk
For historical inquiries and pre-owned sales contact
Graham Greener, W W Greener (Sporting Guns) Limited,
The Mews, Hagley Hall, Hagley, Stourbridge, DY9 9LG, England
01666 510351
sales@wwgreener.com
www.wwgreener.com

Joseph Harkom

Joseph Harkom is today remembered mostly by aficionados of Scottish guns, but in the late nineteenth and early twentieth centuries the maker was renowned for quality, especially for its boxlocks that feature gold-plated internal components, arcaded fences, and a very high level of finish. Joseph Harkom was born in London in 1807 but by 1837 was trading from Leopold Place, in Edinburgh. He eventually moved to more prestigious premises at 32 Princes Street. After the founder's death in 1891, the business was assumed by son Joseph Mark Harkom, who operated it until his death in 1923, trading from 30 George Street. The business was thereafter acquired by Mortimer & Son, also of Edinburgh. In 1938, Mortimer and Harkom were acquired by John Dickson, also of Edinburgh, and integrated into the Dickson business. The Harkom name was subsequently acquired by an avid Harkom collector, and in 1998 the name was obtained by Chris Batha. The latter intends to revive the Harkom name with a line of smallbore round-action bar-in-wood triggerplate guns built on the MacNaughton design.

For Harkom address, *see*
Charles Boswell entry.

Holland & Holland Ltd

Holland & Holland has been described as England's 'most important' sporting gun company. That seems a bold statement, given the quality and contributions of its peers and competitors in London and Birmingham, but taken in overall context the claim to Holland's primacy does not lack merit. The evidence?

Over fifty patents, many of which remain influential – and are widely imitated in the UK and abroad. Among the most important are:

- The Holland Royal side-by-side – the first iteration appearing in 1883 – has long reigned as the world's most copied sidelock. Relatively simple and ultra-reliable, it simply works, and is easier to build, regulate and stock than designs like the Beesley.
- Ejectors: whether known today as 'Southgate' or 'Holland' ejectors, Henry W. Holland's simple two-piece ejector patent of 13 January 1893 works on the over-centre principle and variations of such can be found in almost any double gun worldwide.
- 'Patent Self-Opening Mechanism': appearing in 1922, Holland's spiral-spring-driven device can be fitted to sidelocks and boxlocks alike – and like the 'Royal' remains ubiquitous in use on best guns globally.
- Hand-detachable locks: this 1908-patent thumb lever allows the user to easily remove ('hand-detach') the lockplates. Found today on sidelocks made in Belgium, Spain, Italy, England – and all points between.
- Cartridge technology: Holland & Holland's domination of *The Field's* rifle trials of 1883 showed the shape of things to come in rifle and cartridge development; Holland's 1904 belted rimless cartridge patent gave rise to a host of superb big-bore cartridges, most famously the .375 Holland & Holland – the latter still setting the standard for cartridges of its type.
- The Paradox: this 1885 patent provided for rifling in the choke

area of a shotgun, giving it dual use. Widely copied in its era, the company has recently reintroduced it.

• Over/unders: relatively late players in the best British over/under scene, Holland & Holland's 1991 introduction of the Royal sidelock o/u and 1993's triggerplate 'Sporting' model have helped launch a new generation of English over/unders.

• Engraving: from the introduction of the now-ubiquitous 'Royal' cutaway scroll in the 1890s to the more recent 'Products of Excellence' series, Holland & Holland has influenced fine-gun engraving the world over.

Holland & Holland's manufacturing modes have been likewise influential. With its circa-1898 factory at 906 Harrow Road, Holland & Holland became one of the first London makers to have a purpose-built factory in the fullest sense of the word, complete with machine shop and dedicated equipment. Modernisation in the 1960s helped keep Holland afloat in that difficult decade and through the 1970s, and the firm's 1985 purchase of Birmingham's W. & C. Scott set the stage for the widespread adoption of CAD/CAM technology. However, it was Chanel Ltd's subsequent purchase of Holland & Holland in 1989, which facilitated the sort of investment needed to fully modernise the machine shop to produce all components in-house to Holland's specifications. These capabilities have allowed Holland & Holland to once again bring virtually all of its gunmaking activities in-house, as well as introduce important new models – notably the Royal o/u, the Sporting o/u, as well as a new round-bodied back-action sidelock built in gun, rifle and paradox configurations.

Since the nineties, other English gunmakers have followed Holland's lead – Purdey's, for example, has set up its own CNC machine shop; smaller independent makers have taken the high-tech route by contracting out to speciality machine shops in the automotive and aerospace industries. Regardless, the technological

face of British gunmaking in the early years of the twenty-first century is dramatically different than even a decade ago – and Holland & Holland has unquestionably been a prime mover in that trend.

For more information, contact
Holland & Holland, 33 Bruton Street, London, W1J 6HH
020 7499 4411; fax: 020 7408 7962
gunroomuk@hollandandholland.com
www.hollandandholland.com

Holloway & Naughton

Holloway & Naughton can be traced to the 1870s, when the very young Thomas Naughton entered the Birmingham gun trade during the 1870s. After working with George Bonehill and James Carr, he met G. O'Connor Holloway and began working for, and eventually managing, Holloway & Co. The latter was sold to the owner of the Midland Gun Company but Naughton stayed on and, eventually, in 1909, he purchased the firm and renamed it Holloway & Naughton. As with most Birmingham firms, they made and marketed a wide variety of guns and rifles to both the trade and to retail customers – and was particularly known for its pigeon guns. It remained in Naughton family hands until being acquired by F.J. Wiseman in the early 1950s. Given the torpor of the trade in the post-war era, Holloway & Naughton's name remained mostly dormant until 1992, when it was resuscitated by a partnership between Wiseman and Andrew Harvison, the latter a former shooting grounds owner, and champion skeet and sporting shooter. The goal was to design and bring to market an innovative best-quality British over/under suitable for sustained use. The Wiseman/Harvison partnership ended in 2003 with Harvison retaining title to the Holloway & Naughton name for the production of sidelock o/us and side-by-sides, along with sporting rifles built in a number of configurations. According to Harvison, the severance agreement allows Wiseman to make boxlocks under the Holloway & Naughton name.

Harvison has since assembled a team of top British craftsmen and is currently making best-quality Boss-type over/unders and Purdey/Beesley-type side-by-sides. The latest offering is a proprietary o/u design – the Britannia – initially built as a sideplated triggerplate gun but which has since evolved to a sidelock design. It is less complex (and expensive) than the Boss gun, and the Britannia's CNC production and contemporary metallurgy bode well for reliability.

For more information on Holloway & Naughton guns, contact Andrew Harvison, Turners Barn Farm, Kibworth Road Three Gates, Billesdon, Leicestershire LE7 9EQ, England
0116 259 6592
afharvision@hollowaynaughton.co.uk
www.hollowaynaughton.co.uk

William Palmer Jones

Today few know the name of Birmingham's William Palmer Jones but almost any serious shotgun shooter is familiar with the try gun – his most durable and influential invention.

Born in 1845, from a line of established Birmingham gunmakers, Jones eventually assumed control of the family firm that bore the family name. Throughout his career he was granted seven patents, including 1888's Patent No. 17732 (Plate 69). The most lasting of these, however, came in 1889 with Patent No. 1157 of 22 January for a 'try gun'. Another version came later that year with Patent No. 5372 of 29 March. Try guns existed before Jones's version but none were as sophisticated and adaptable as his. The invention was important enough that Jones named his factory on Whittal Street the 'Try Gun Works'. Other inventions included targets, target-throwing devices, cartridge-loading machines, shot-counting devices, and a single

trigger in 1895 – No. 5543 of 16 March, co-patented with William Baker, another of Birmingham's most inventive makers. Jones was active and prominent within the Birmingham trade, serving as a Guardian of the Proof House. He died in 1920, although the business apparently continued until the mid-1970s.

Charles Lancaster & Co.

Charles Lancaster the founder began as a barrelmaker to the best London trade in the early years of the nineteenth century, supplying the likes of Purdey and both Manton brothers. He opened his own business on 151 New Bond Street in 1826, urged on by Col. Peter Hawker, a proponent of his skills. Lancaster died in 1847, but not before garnering Prince Albert's Royal warrant. Son Charles William was a talented craftsman in his own right and continued the business, along with brother Alfred, and the Lancaster name was renowned by the mid-nineteenth century for its innovations, especially in rifling – the 'Oval Bore' being a notable example. Lancaster also built multi-barrel guns in many configurations, and pioneered early British breechloaders and cartridge development. After the death of Charles William in 1878, the firm passed into the hands of assistant Henry A.A. Thorn, who thereafter dubbed himself 'Mr Charles Lancaster' and changed the firm's name to Charles Lancaster & Co. A colourful, controversial figure in his day, Thorn remains well known for his book *The Art of Shooting* (published under the pseudonym Charles Lancaster and still in print), as well as his efforts to make and promote multi-barrel firearms. He also patented single triggers and ejectors, introduced the 2-inch 'Pygmy' cartridge, and developed a spring-opening gun better known as the 'wrist-breaker' due to the efforts needed to close it. Thorn died in 1914, with son George Frederick managing the business until his death in 1920. In the mid-1920s, Lancaster introduced its 'Twelve-Twenty' best lightweight sidelock –

and Lancaster's name became synonymous with it – though it was made on the 1913 design of Birmingham's William Baker. The Depression, however, proved the firm's undoing, and in 1932 the assets were sold to Stephen Grant & Joseph Lang and the name amalgamated. The Baker-action 'Twelve-Twenty' continued to be marketed under the Lancaster name, and also as Grant's 'Lightweight'. After Atkin Grant & Lang stopped trading in 1980, the Charles Lancaster & Co. name was decoupled and sold and gunmaking revived. Of late, the Lancaster business was purchased by Francis Beardsworth and Ron Wharton, the latter a Rigby-trained gunmaker with a speciality in rifles. According to Wharton the firm is currently making double rifles and sidelock shotguns, as well as bolt rifles.

For more information, contact

Charles Lancaster & Co. Ltd, Rhome Cottage, Capel Road, Rusper, Horsham, West Sussex, RH12 4PZ

01293 871453; fax. 01293 871379

www.charleslancastergunmakers.co.uk

Wharton@bunduki.co.uk

Joseph Lang

One of the more salient cultural aspects of British gunmaking is not only its long and illustrious history, but also its obsession with that history. Whereas many of the Continent's finest craftsmen begin their histories afresh by starting companies under their own names, more common in Britain is the everlasting use of monikers belonging to influential (if long dead) makers from the past. Joseph Lang – in many permutations through two centuries – provides a prime example.

The original Joseph Lang was a gifted craftsman who founded his business in London in 1821, and in 1828 married one of James Purdey's daughters. As a gunmaker, however, he secured his fame by helping introduce the breechloading sporting gun to Britain after encountering a French Lefaucheux pinfire at the Great Exhibition of 1851. Lang the Founder died in 1868 and in 1875 the name was changed to Joseph Lang & Son, with son James and stepmother carrying on the business. Lang's history becomes astonishingly convoluted thereafter, with James departing in 1886 to establish his own business, which eventually became Lang & Hussey Ltd in 1894 (with the capable rogue H.J. Hussey at the helm). Joseph Lang & Son, in the meantime, had been sold in 1886 and was eventually purchased by Birmingham's P. Webley in 1893. Joseph Lang & Son was then amalgamated with Lang & Hussey Ltd in 1898, with the Webley family as major shareholders. Hussey was soon booted under suspicion of embezzlement, and the name changed to Joseph Lang & Son Ltd. The firm carried on until 1915, when the effects of the war forced it into liquidation. In 1917, Joseph Lang & Son Ltd was reformed, and it survived alone until 1925, when William Robson, new owner of Stephen Grant & Sons, purchased the Lang business and amalgamated it as Stephen Grant & Joseph Lang.

Today, current Atkin Grant & Lang owner Ken Duglan, has made a speciality of restoring guns originally built by the London trio. Lang sidelocks of modern configuration–that is, with bar-action locks and Southgate-type ejectors–make excellent restoration projects due to their original quality and soundness of design. Duglan also regards Lang's trigger of 1901 as reliable for those seeking a single-trigger gun.

See Stephen Grant chapter for more information.

G.E. Lewis/John Harris

Guns bearing the name G.E. Lewis have been built since at least 1850, when the founder of the same name opened shop on Lower Loveday Street, in Birmingham's gun quarter. Like many makers in the city, Lewis built guns to a wide variety of prices and quality, and in a great many configurations – from the ultra-lightweight 'Ariel' model meant to compete with Churchill's XXVs to heavy fowlers. The company remained in family hands until the late 1980s, when the last G.E. Lewis died. The business was subsequently obtained in 1989 by John Harris (born 1941 in Shipston-on-Stour), a master gunmaker with a speciality in stocking.

Harris entered the Birmingham gun trade in 1970, where he worked for Benjamin Wild & Sons for four years before setting up on his own in the former S. Wrights/Churchill workshop at 98 Bath Street. He principally worked as a stocker to the trade for the first decade, before taking on some private customers. In 1992 he moved shop to 63 Price Street, leaving in the late nineties to work from his home.

For the last twenty years his forte has been stocking best sidelocks, some for London's finest makers. In his career he also made twenty-two guns, including eight under the G.E. Lewis name – such as the 4-bore (Plate 75). Harris sold the Lewis name in 2003 at Holt's Auctioneers and is today semi-retired. (Contact details for John Harris unpublished at his request.)

George MacFarlaine

Engineer-turned-gunmaker George MacFarlaine turned out a handful of three-barrelled guns built to his designs in the 1990s.

Born in India in 1930, MacFarlaine was raised in a sporting family and in the 1960s moved from India to the Lake District, where he established MacFarlaine Sports, a supplier of shooting supplies and equipment. An avid shooter, MacFarlaine's passion was collecting unusual guns – including three- and four-barrel examples by various British and Continental makers. An engineer by training, his ultimate ambition was to make multi-barrel guns, and he stripped and studied examples from his own collection to evaluate the Victorian-era designs. His own efforts began when a fourth-generation gunmaking family

hosted his daughter on an exchange visit to Ferlach, Austria. Thus introduced to the Ferlach trade – with its tradition of building multi-barrel guns – MacFarlaine investigated a variety of Austrian designs. He eventually settled on a three-barrelled design – believing a quad-barrel gun too heavy and complex for field shooting. His first project was a 10-bore three-barrel built on a Ferlach-machined frame with Boehler-steel tubes, with MacFarlaine fitting and regulating the components. He picked the 10-bore because the components were large and easier to work with. A triggerplate design was used, and proved easiest to mate with an inertia-regulated single trigger. The barrels were configured two-over-one, providing the shooter a conventional view. MacFarlaine later turned his attention to a 20-bore version and completed several guns before his death in 2000. His family continues the business today under the name 'The Sporting Lodge'.

For more information, contact
The Sporting Lodge, Storth, Milnthorpe, Cumbria, LA7 7JA
01539 563594
www.thesportinglodge.co.uk
enquiries@thesportinglodge.co.uk

James MacNaughton

Little has been published of James MacNaughton's early life but he is first recorded in 1864 as making guns on Edinburgh's George Street. His 'Lockfast Breech Loader' was introduced in the late 1860s, a slide-and-drop action, but in 1879 he patented his most important design: 'The Edinburgh Gun'. The earliest of the Scottish triggerplate Round Actions, the first versions were cocked by a long pierced toplever but the design matured to a conventional barrel-cocking version fitted with standard toplever. His guns received critical acclaim, taking a gold medal at the Melbourne exposition in 1881 and in 1886 winning another gold at the Edinburgh Exposition. In 1890 he patented ejectors for the guns, and followed this with patents for rifle sights. MacNaughton died in 1905 in his mid-sixties; around this time he was operating a shop in Perth, as well as on Edinburgh's Hanover Street, remaining in the latter premises until the 1940s. In 1947, rival John Dickson acquired MacNaughton and amalgamated it, but continued to build a few MacNaughton-badged guns until the 1950s.

With vintage Round Action guns in high demand, the MacNaughton name was revived in 1995 when Scottish landowner Alistair Lang and partners purchased it from Dickson with the idea of restarting gun production. Then, in 1999, MacNaughton's new owners purchased Dickson, and the firm was renamed Dickson & MacNaughton, and it today trades from Dickson's historic Frederick Street premises.

For further details *see* Dickson entry.

Mike Marsh

Open the oak and leather case of almost any new best British gun and chances are it will be fitted out with the finely crafted tools and accessories of Mike Marsh.

Marsh was born in 1942 in Derbyshire, and grew up shooting and fishing. Upon leaving school he served a six-year apprenticeship in engineering, followed by a career as an instrument maker in Sheffield, at the time still known for its cutlery and hand-tool manufacture.

In the early seventies, Marsh became interested in muzzle-loading, and made a powder flask – the quality of which attracted, in his words, 'considerable interest'. Within a couple years he began making powder flasks commercially, closely copying the nineteenth century flasks of Sheffield's G. & J.W. Hawksley. He began making accessories in 1982, after realising the demand for high-quality tools for casing best guns.

Marsh's tools are inspired by vintage designs, and he works with traditional materials – horn and ebony for handles, nickel silver joints and ferules, and tool steel for turnscrew blades. All are made by Marsh alone in his workshop, in which he has accrued 'a vast quantity of gauges, patterns and jigs'. Almost all his work has been for the gun trade, though he is currently working to produce a field-cleaning kit bearing his name. Although Marsh has reached retirement age, he admits to a 'vast backlog' of work and notes he will probably never fully retire. (Contact details withheld at Mike Marsh's request.)

Alexander Martin

Alexander Martin was founded in Paisley, Scotland in 1837. In the nineteenth century, Martin was well known for its association with rifle regulation and target shooting. Shotguns with beautifully executed Celtic engraving were offered and Martin made a speciality of 'Ribless' guns. By the mid-twentieth century these were made in Birmingham, with A.A. Brown & Sons producing many of the 'Ribless' guns.

One of the firm's most lasting modern legacies was launching the career of David McKay Brown, who joined the firm in 1958 as an apprentice shortly before the company was sold to John Dickson & Sons. New Martin guns are again being sold; in the last decade Dickson & MacNaughton have marketed Italian-made *(Wifra Armi)* and Italian-engraved *(Cesare Giovanelli)* triggerplate guns under the banner of 'Alex Martin Continentals'.

For more information, *see* John Dickson & Son Ltd history.

P.V. Nelson (Gunmakers)

His closest friends call him 'Victor' to others he is 'Mr Perfection'. Whatever the name, Peter Victor Nelson is recognised by gun connoisseurs as one of the world's finest gunmakers. Though his

Custom case by Vince Rickard for a set of four Peter Nelson guns with tools by Mike Marsh.

clientele is small in numbers – almost all Americans – they are the world's most important collectors, and the guns Nelson has built for them have served as a canvas for the world's finest engravers. Many of Nelson's peers (as well as his clients) credit his uncompromising standards of excellence for helping revive 'best quality' craftsmanship in the London trade – standards which had suffered at many firms following the Second World War. Notes one client who has ordered forty (yes, forty) of his guns: 'There is a real legacy in the standards that Peter set that other makers aspired to, and that *definitely* increased quality in the contemporary high-end gun market.'

Nelson, born in 1938 in Acton, London, started gunmaking in 1953 at James Purdey & Sons, where at age fifteen he was apprenticed to Ernie Lawrence as an actioner. He remained at Purdey until 1971, when he left to join Germany's Hartmann & Weiss, in Hamburg, where Nelson helped make rifles and the Beesley action self-openers he had made at Purdey. During his eighteen-year relationship with the firm, Nelson built six rifles and twenty-six side-by-sides. In 1989, he left to build guns under his own name from his own workshop. Since then he has delivered forty-three side-by-side guns – most of them Boss- or Beesley/Purdey-type guns. Three of these were made on true spring-opening Boss-type actions, always an ultra-rare design. Over/unders completed total thirty-six, all of them to the Boss system. He has also built three side-by-side double rifles on either Boss-type side-by-side and two on Boss over/under actions.

Astonishingly these guns have been built for only nine customers, with two of them ordering over sixty P. V. Nelson guns between them. Nelson once estimated he would spend three times as long building a gun with his own name on it than he had under the employ of others. Most have been engraved by English masters such as Ken Hunt, Alan and Paul Brown, Phil Coggan and Keith Thomas. At age seventy-one, Nelson's career is by his own admission winding down but one suspects retirement is not in his plans. (Address withheld at P. V. Nelson's request.)

William Powell & Sons

Sometimes dubbed the 'Purdey's of Birmingham', William Powell & Sons has been one the city's most prestigious gunmakers for more than two centuries. What is all the more astounding is that it remained in the founding family hands for more than two centuries until 2008, when brothers Peter and David Powell sold the business to former Churchill co-owner Mark Osbourne, who has relocated the business from its long-time home on Carrs Lane in central Birmingham to more gunshop-friendly Banbury, in Oxfordshire.

Powell's founding dates to 1802 when the first William Powell entered into a partnership with Joseph Simmons. Upon the latter's death in 1812, Powell became sole proprietor and a Birmingham gunmaking dynasty began. Unlike many Birmingham firms – which largely built guns anonymously for the trade – Powell successfully established a retail business early on, and its guns have been distinguished by understated elegance and superb craftsmanship. At least 12,000 sporting arms have been built, a testament to the firm's reputation. Powell's introduced several successful patents in the nineteenth century, the best known of which is the 'Lift Uplever' as seen on Plate 96.

Successive generations of Powells have served the gun trade by taking leadership roles with the Birmingham Gun Barrel Proof House, the latest being Peter Powell, who was elected Guardian in 1975. After serving as the Guardian's chairman of finance and vice-chairman for two decades, he was elected chairman in 1995, and served in that position until 2005. He subsequently retired but was asked to remain on the board as deputy chairman.

For more information, contact

William Powell & Son, Carrs House, 1 Tramway, Banbury,

Oxfordshire, OX16 5TD

01295 701701

www.william-powell.co.uk

James Purdey & Sons

There is some room for argument over who is Britain's best gunmaker – but Britain's best gunmaking name clearly belongs to James Purdey & Sons. 'Purdey' is today synonymous with best quality – as it was through the nineteenth and twentieth centuries – and as a luxury brand it transcends the gunmaking trade into larger public consciousness in a way that only Holland & Holland can rival.

James Purdey the founder (born 1784) completed his apprenticeship in 1805 and went to work for Joseph Manton, with his mentor famously remarking after Purdey had left in 1814 to establish his own business: 'Purdey gets up the best work next to mine.'

Unlike Manton, who was soon destined for bankruptcy, Purdey went on to found an enduring commercial dynasty. In an intensely competitive era riven by class-consciousness, patronage from the proper social strata was crucial to success, and the quality of Purdey's guns soon attracted the aristocracy at home and abroad. In 1823 Purdey made its first gun for Continental royalty and two years later for the Duke of Gloucester, brother to King George IV. By 1838, Queen Victoria was a customer, and since that time Purdey has supplied the royal family. By the early twentieth century, the firm could boast of being a gunmaker to all nine crowned heads of Europe. Even today, Purdey still holds royal warrants from HM The Queen, HRH The Duke of Edinburgh, and HRH The Prince of Wales.

Great gunmaking, of course, was the key to attracting and retaining this sort of patronage. Throughout its history, the firm was granted sixteen patents, the most enduring being 1863's double-bolt snap action – in essence the famed 'Purdey underbolt' which secures the barrels to action of almost every side-by-side double gun made in the world today. If successive generations of Purdey gunmakers proved more conservative in invention than some of their peers, they have had an uncanny ability to recognise merits in the designs of others, and to turn those merits to their advantage.

Notably this includes Frederick Beesley's 1879 invention of the self-opening action, which Purdey purchased from the former in 1880 – and has since become the basis for the firm's best-quality side-by-sides. It took another two-thirds of a century to obtain an over/under equivalent, but the 1948 purchase of James Woodward & Sons secured for Purdey a great over/under, and more than five hundred best o/us have since been made to a slightly modified Woodward design.

For much of the twentieth century the British gun trade was plagued by contraction and amalgamation. Possession of seminal gun designs and Purdey's unquestioned legacy helped it survive wars and subsequent economic dislocations but it was really a massive capital infusion following the 1994 acquisition by Vendome PLC, a French luxury goods consortium, that launched another golden age of gunmaking at Audley House.

Purdey's has subsequently modernised its machine shop and under the energetic leadership of Richard Purdey (grandson of James Purdey IV) and Nigel Beaumont (a bench-trained gunmaker) the firm began to claw back the stunning quality and vision that established its reputation. Not only do many knowledgeable observers today regard today's guns as the best the firm has ever built, but Purdeys are available in variety not seen since the late nineteenth century. Actions are now available in a range of shapes: traditional, semi-round, and ultraround; guns have been re-engineered and scaled to appropriate sizes per bore; bar-action hammerguns and Woodward models have been reintroduced; and a new triggerplate over/under launched at a more accessible price.

All is evidence that there is more to Purdey's fame than its name.

For more information, contact

James Purdey & Sons, Audley House, 57 - 58 South Audley Street, London W1K 2ED

020 7499 1801; fax:020 7355 3297

enquiries@purdey.com

www.purdey.com

Westley Richards & Co.

British gunmaking is sometimes deemed old-fashioned but it is well worth remembering that a century ago it was regarded as anything but.

In the three and a half decades preceding the twentieth century, breechloading – then hammerless – side-by-side guns were perfected in a wide variety of designs. Innovation had sprung from all quarters in Britain but arguably most abundantly from gunmaker Westley Richards. Company literature of the time touted the firm's 'modern' approach to gunmaking and its 'progressive spirit' and, in both cases, it wasn't marketing hype.

Since its founding in Birmingham in 1812, Westley had pushed the boundaries of firearms technology, introducing notable improvements in percussion, breechloading and military gunmaking, as well as with ammunition.

With their revolutionary patent of 1875, Westley's William Anson and John Deeley had created the genesis for the modern sporting shotgun – a gun with concealed hammers as well as locks that cocked with the fall of the barrels. The firm's doll's-head top extension and bolting system were enormously influential, its mechanical single trigger and ejector systems proven, and its forend fasteners were (and still are) trade standards. Westley's detachable locks – more commonly known in America today as 'droplocks' – were nothing short of genius. Westley's over/under of 1914 – the Ovundo – was a final flourish of gunmaking innovation at the firm.

Unlike much of the Birmingham trade, which typically relied on a network of outworkers, Westley's was mostly a self-contained operation with its own dedicated factory, and the firm took great pride in building guns to its own designs, guns made with every intention of competing with those of London. The First World War brought all this to a halt.

Unlike some Birmingham firms, however, Westley entered the post-1914 years healthier than many of its competitors. For one, it was positioned to tap a burgeoning American market and, most importantly, the patronage of fabulously wealthy Indian princes.

The 1930s, on the other hand, ushered in tougher times and the Second World War essentially wrecked a firm dependent on a rapidly shrinking empire. Captain E.D. Barclay purchased the bankrupt business from liquidators in 1946 and Westley muddled through another decade before being sold to Captain Walter Clode in 1957. The latter kept Westley's gunmaking going through some lean years – largely through repairs and renovation to second-hand guns he was buying from the armouries of Indian princes – but in the meantime he concentrated efforts on modernising the firm's hi-tech engineering and toolmaking operations. It was a move that would return dividends when his son Simon Clode joined in 1987.

Simon integrated the CNC millers, spark-eroders and wire cutters of Westley's engineering division with the files and chisels of its bench-trained craftsmen. At the time the gun Westley was best known for, its hand-detachable droplock side-by-side, was still being made in 12-gauge, but only sporadically and by hand and virtually on a one-off basis, making it very costly and inefficient to produce. Simon's goal was to bring the detachable-lock back into regular production, using the latest manufacturing technology married to traditional gunmaking skills. In the late 1980s he launched this process with the .410 version, only six of which had ever been made. Ten were initially produced to great success, and since then Westley has followed up with 28-, 16-, 20-, 12-, 10-gauges (even an 8-bore is currently under construction), as well as building it in a host of rifle calibres. All are built on scaled frames appropriate to each gauge or calibre.

With the hand-detachable back as its core product, Westley also now makes bolt rifles, standard Anson & Deeley boxlock rifles, sidelock shotguns and rifles, the newly reintroduced 'Ovundo' over/under, as well as its own proprietary rifle ammunition. Under Clode's tutelage it has also diversified into making its own best-quality gun cases and leather goods. Virtually everything, save the ammunition, is made in-house.

Modern engineering has been integrated into the gunmaking process but Clode has deliberately restrained it from fully supplanting traditional craft. 'Our machinery could make a new gun to near-finished specs,' Clode says, 'but then you quickly lose traditional gunmaking skills. Once those skills are gone they are gone for good.' This vision and Westley's unique guns, and the quality to which they are made, have garnered Clode a loyal and discerning clientele base as impressive as any since the halcyon days of the Empire. Among them number not only the bulk of the world's most prominent collectors but also kings and princes from across the globe.

Founder William Westley Richards had a simple motto: 'To make as good a gun as can be made.' In that regard, nothing has changed at Westley Richards.

For more information, contact
Westley Richards & Co. Ltd, 130 Pritchett Street,
Birmingham B6 4EH, England
0121 333 1900; fax: 0121 333 1901
sales@westleyrichards.co.uk
www.westleyrichards.com

David H. Sinnerton

David Sinnerton is today England's most famous finisher to the trade. He is also now a gunmaker, building best sidelock over/unders and side-by-sides under his own name.

Sinnerton was born in London in 1959 and joined Purdey as an apprentice at age sixteen in 1976. Apprenticed to Robert (Bob) Nicholls, he joined the Purdey finishing shop, where he worked for twelve years before leaving in 1988 to set up as a freelance finisher to the trade. He has never lacked for work since, thanks to a hard-earned reputation for excellence and a peerless work ethic. Trade clients have included the cream of British gunmaking – Purdey, Boss & Co. and Peter V. Nelson, among others – as well as restoration and repair work for retail buyers and the trade. He built his first gun under his own name in 1992, a 12-bore Purdey/Beesley self-opener, as a gift for his father. The first retail orders for Sinnerton-badged guns came in 2001, and he has since built best sidelock side-by-sides on both Holland and Purdey/Beesley actions, as well as over/unders on Boss-type actions. He now lives and works in West Sussex.

> For more information contact the maker at
> 01798 813849 or
> *davidsinnerton@aol.com*

C.H. Smith & Sons

One of the oldest firms operating in what remains of the old Birmingham gun quarter is C.H. Smith & Sons, founded by Charles Hubert Smith, in 1840. Long a fixture on Steelhouse Lane, Smith moved to Price Street in 1984. In recent decades, the founder's grandson, Gordon Smith made a speciality of barrel-boring for the trade, although the firm also performs general servicing and refurbishment. Gordon's widow, Mary, noted that her late husband began barrel-boring when it was not being performed elsewhere to Smith's standards. Gordon purchased a honing machine and made his own tools and the quality of his work was such that he was soon boring barrels for others. The high standards he brought to his craft are evident in boxlock No. 28788 (Plate 124). Gordon died in 2006 aged seventy-four. Mary continues to operate Smith with business partner Brian Bateman.

> For more information, contact
> C.H. Smith & Sons, Unit GF 1, 63 Price Street, Birmingham,
> England, B4 6JZ
> 0121 359 1680

Mark W. Sullivan, with John Craven and Colin Orchard

Since the early 1990s, actioner Mark William Sullivan and a team of outworkers allied with him have been responsible for building, or helping to build, many of the best sidelocks to have come out of smaller London gunmakers that do not possess their own workshops or full teams of in-house craftsmen. Sullivan, born in London in 1958, became interested in guns through his father, a shooter. He joined Holland & Holland aged sixteen as an apprentice, working under the guidance of Stan Robinson, before transferring to Holland's action shop to complete his five-year apprenticeship. In 1989, following the Chanel takeover, he left Holland & Holland to set up as an outworker to the trade, along with a number of other ex-Holland craftsmen, including fellow actioner John Craven, finisher Colin Orchard, stocker Chris Whaley, and engravers Alan Portsmouth and Peter Ashford. About ninety per cent of their early work was taken by Asprey, which had opened its gunroom in 1990. The team has also built guns for Rigby (Paul Roberts), Atkin Grant & Lang, Beesley, Symes & Wright, Charles Boswell, and others. Today, the heart of the gunmaking team remains together – Sullivan, Craven (born in London 1961) and Orchard (born in London in 1960) – with most of current production going to William Asprey's William & Son. French-born stocker Stephane Dupille (ex-Holland & Holland and Watson Bros) and barrelmaker Mick Kelly (ex-Purdey) round out today's team.

Although Sullivan and company specialise (not surprisingly) in classic Holland & Holland 'Royal'-type sidelock side-by-sides, they have also made sidelever Grants for Atkin Grant & Lang, and a handful of big-bore double rifles. In 2004, Sullivan introduced a proprietary best sidelock over/under, which is available through William & Son. Sullivan has not made guns under his name for retail customers – and admits he is happier avoiding the limelight by working for the trade – but his team's production is characterised by exceptional quality and a work ethic that takes quiet pride in its training, skills and craftsmanship.

For more information, contact
William & Son.

Robert E. Turner/Turner Richards (Gunmakers)

The history of the British gun trade brims with brilliant craftsmen whose names today are lost to time – their legacy preserved, if only anonymously, in the surviving guns they once helped make. In an earlier age, gunmaker Robert Edward Turner would have provided a perfect example of such.

Turner, born in 1939 in Birmingham, has spent nearly all his fifty-year career out of the limelight, instead making guns for some of Britain's best makers. 'Ninety-nine per cent of my work has been for the trade,' said Turner. 'No, make that 99.9 per cent.' Not only is Turner a craftsman in the traditional sense, but he is also an accomplished engineer and gun designer, as proficient in computer-aided design and manufacture as he is with a chisel and file.

Born within a mile of Westley Richards's historic factory, Turner launched his career in the mid-1950s not in gunmaking but in the machine-tool trade, where he learned machining, precision-fitting and, later, engineering design and drafting. Fascinated by guns since childhood, he spent spare time at the Westley Richards factory, where 'the old hands', as Turner called them, taught him the craft of gunmaking, with Harry Payne – one of Westley's most accomplished craftsmen – becoming his mentor. Turner proved an adept student and was soon doing odd jobs for the trade. His first big break was machining Westley's 'One Trigger' single-trigger components, then building and regulating it for the company. Given the Westley trigger's complexity, and the precision and skill needed to make it, this was no mean feat. Gunmaking remained a part-time occupation until 1973, when Turner left the machine-tool trade to set up on his own in Bromsgrove. Several years later he was approached by William Powell & Sons to assist in making its best sidelocks. Other gunmakers he built sidelocks for included the makers in the Atkin Grant & Lang stable and other smaller London and provincial makers. 'For about twenty years I also made both single- and double-trigger furniture for Boss & Co.,' Turner added. 'I also made double rifles for Danl. Fraser. I finished some of these rifles with the Asprey of London name.'

In the late 1990s Turner was approached by Scotland's James MacNaughton, which at the time was attempting to revive its gun production, using its famous 'Edinburgh Gun' as a springboard. Turner was given the task of redesigning and re-engineering the gun in both bar-in-wood and solid-body versions, in 12- and 20-bore. Similar work followed for the Round Action when MacNaughton purchased Dickson in 1999.

It was not until 2002 that he began his first gun for a private customer under the Turner Richards Gunmaker's name, the latter name retained from a past partnership with Ken Richardson (also of W.W. Greener Ltd). Since 1985, Turner has also served as a Guardian for the Birmingham Proof House. At age seventy-one Turner admits the bulk of his career on the bench is behind him but he still actively designs guns and components at his workshop in Bromsgrove.

For more information, contact
bob.sidelock@btinternet.com

Watson Bros

A century ago, London's Watson Bros carved out a niche in a crowded and competitive marketplace by specialising in smallbore doubles during the era when the 12-bore reigned supreme. Today Watson Bros has created another niche, this time by building sleek and slender 12-bore over/unders that weigh the same as, and handle like, classic British side-by-side game guns.

The firm harkens to 1875, when Thomas William Watson began trading at 4 Pall Mall. In 1884/85, the firm became Watson Bros, named after Thomas William and brother Arthur Henry, and subsequently courted a reputation as London's specialist for smallbore guns. In 1933 Thomas William died and in 1935 Arthur Henry retired, and the assets were purchased by W. Robson of Stephen Grant & Joseph Lang Ltd. Some guns continued to be built under the Watson name, mostly smallbores. In 1984, the owners of Churchill, Atkin Grant & Lang sold C. Hellis, F. Beesley and Watson names to Frederick Buller, of Amersham.

In 1989, a young Purdey-trained gunmaker named Michael Louca (born 1960, in east London), purchased the largely dormant name from Buller, with the idea of rebuilding the marque and making guns to his own vision. Louca's idea was to make new Watsons as slender, round-body sidelocks that, while paying homage to the great designs of the past, were copies of none of them. His goal was also to build them, as much as possible, under one roof by in-house craftsmen.

He assembled a small team, trained by the likes of craftsmen from Boss's, Holland and Purdey, and in 1992 rented workshop space on the upper floor of an old printer's facility at 39 Redcross Way, just south of London Bridge. Watson concentrated first on developing smallbore sidelock side-by-sides built on the Beesley/Purdey self-opening action but aesthetically as sleek as a Boss round-body. Through the late 1990s Louca and his staff also worked on perfecting a new lightweight over/under, based loosely on the Woodward/Purdey design but made with a proprietary ejector system that allowed Watson to trim both the size of the forend and action, and also reduce its weight. In 2001, Louca declared the new ejector 'perfected' and Watson's lightweight o/us have given it a unique market niche and have proved popular – even in 12-bore configurations. Although smallbores were once most popular at Watson, today's customer is most likely to order a trim 12-bore o/u. Louca has also seen increased demand, conversely, for heavier, high-pheasant configurations.

Unafraid to tackle the unusual, Watson is also building a three-barrel hybrid sidelock/triggerplate side-by-side-by-side and several 4-bores. In October 2006 Louca moved Watson Bros to 54 Redchurch Street, in the Shoreditch district of East London.

Watson Bros remains one of the few independent gunmakers to recruit and train new craftsmen. Craftsmen currently on-staff that have been trained by Louca include Ryan Glyde (barrelmaker) and Brad Hodgson (ejectorwork). Also working in-house at present are Leanne Green (engraver) and trainee James Brown.

For more information, contact
Watson Bros Gunmakers, c/o Michael Louca, 54 Redchurch Street, London E2 7DP
0207 033 0003
www.watsonbrosgunmakers.com
Michael.Louca@WatsonBrosGunMakers.com

T.R. White & Co.

Tony R. White was born in Birmingham in 1958 and joined Webley & Scott in 1974. Trained at Scott as a stocker and finisher, he was one of the few craftsmen retained when Holland & Holland purchased the Birmingham firm in 1985, which by then was trading under the W. & C. Scott banner. In 1989 he went independent, though he continued to help build the 'Cavalier' boxlock for Holland & Holland for several years until the latter discontinued it. Assembling a team of craftsmen–barrelmaker John Chandler (ex-Scott and Holland & Holland group), actioner Ted Atkinson (ex-Scott, Holland & Holland group, and Westley Richards), and colour-hardener Bill Lane (ex-Scott and Holland & Holland group). White relocated his workshop on the Shugborough shooting grounds on Lord Lichfield's estate near Stafford in Staffordshire in

1995. T.R. White & Co. made its reputation by specialising in high-quality Anson & Deeley boxlocks, the ubiquitous design virtually abandoned by the rest of the British gun trade by the end of the twentieth century.

The firm also developed a triggerplate over/under, and has since moved into making sidelock over/unders and side-by-sides. Chandler and Lane have since retired but Atkinson (born 1948) remains with White at Shugborough. Along with A.A. Brown & Sons, White & Co. remains one of the few independent gunmakers to colour-case-harden its own work. In addition to its work for retail customers, White has built guns in the past – many of them boxlocks – for Thomas Bland, Cogswell & Harrison and Holland & Holland.

For more information, contact

T.R. White & Co., The Old Barn, Shugborough Shooting School, Oakedge Park, Wolseley Bridge, nr Stafford, ST17 OXS

01889 881661; fax 01889 883038

Tony.White30@btinternet.com

William & Son

The founding of the firm that today trades as William & Son dates to only 1999, but the initial chapter in its story began more than two centuries ago. The first 'William' was William Asprey, a calico printer of Huguenot descent, who opened shop in 1781 and laid the foundations for a firm that would thereafter bear the Asprey family name. By the mid-nineteenth century, and into the twentieth, the London-based company expanded into almost every facet of the luxury trades, and with notable success – in case and cabinet-making, gold and silversmithing, watchmaking, leather goods and luggage, and, of course, jewellery. Asprey did so by buying out its competitors and appropriating their expertise and product line. By the Edwardian

era the terms 'Asprey's' and 'luxury goods' were almost synonomous. Adding gunmaking to the stable, however, did not occur until 1989, when the Asprey family turned its acquisition strategy to Holland & Holland Ltd, which at the time was attempting to fend off a number of unsolicited takeover attempts.

Chanel's successful bid for Holland & Holland proved only a temporary halt to Asprey's aspiration and in 1990 the company unveiled the Asprey Gun Room. It proved a success from the beginning, partly because of the prestige inherent in the Asprey name but also because a top-notch gunmaking team had been found to back the brand's centuries-old reputation. Six Holland & Holland craftsmen were contracted to work exclusively on new Asprey guns (see Mark Sullivan chapter for more information). The same year William Asprey, a seventh-generation direct-descendant of the company's founder, joined Asprey and by 1994 was working in the gun room. Scott Luard joined that year as well and the pair worked together promoting Asprey guns even after the 1995 buyout of the company by Prince Jefri Bolkiah, younger brother of the Sultan of Brunei, and its 1998 merger with London jeweller Garrard.

In 1999 William and Scott struck out on their own and formed a separate business – W.R.A. (Guns) Ltd, which would trade under the name 'William R Asprey Esq.'. In September 2000 the company moved to 10 Mount Street but the emegence of a new firm with the Asprey name did not please the owners of Asprey & Garrard and the latter took legal procedings against WRA (Guns) Ltd for 'passing off' and for infringement of the 'Asprey' trademark. The court ruled with Asprey & Garrard and in 2002 the firm's trading name was officially changed to William & Son. (Ironically, Asprey has since closed its gunroom.)

In 2005, William & Son moved its gunroom to a dedicated showroom at 14 Mount Street, while retaining the 10 Mount Street shop for its line of luxury goods. At present the team of gunmakers used by William & Son still includes a number of craftsmen who signed on with Asprey – notably Mark Sullivan, John Craven and Colin Orchard. Barrelmaker Mick Kelly (ex-Purdey) and actioner Gary Hibbert (ex-Holland & Holland) round out the current team. Paul West (ex-Holland & Holland) works in-house at Mount Street and helps supervise production. In addition, the services of a number of stockers and engravers are also used.

For more information, contact
William & Son, 14 Mount Street, London, W1K 2RF
020 7493 8385
info@williamandson.com
www.williamandson.com

James Woodward & Sons

In the summer of 1948, an aging Charles F. Woodward, of James Woodward & Sons, approached Tom Purdey with a simple request: buy my business. As the fourth member of the top tier of London firms – Boss & Co., Holland & Holland, and Purdey being the others–Woodward wanted its over/under to remain in production, though only if its quality was retained. In C.F. Woodward's estimation, only James Purdey & Sons could build it properly. In September 1948 the deal was sealed, and since then Purdey has built all of its sidelock over/unders on a slightly modified Woodward design.

Along with the Boss, the Woodward is one of the world's seminal over/unders – and ranks as one of Britain's greatest gun designs ever. The gun was launched in 1913, and from then until July 1948 records indicate the firm made about 228 'Under & Over' guns, according to Purdey's Peter Blaine. This is a small production number for such an influential design, but the Woodward o/u was always a complex and costly gun to build.

Jame Woodward the founder had been born in 1815 and had joined Charles Moore to form Moore & Woodward in 1844. In 1872, the name changed to James Woodward & Sons, when sons James and Charles joined. Over the next half century the firm forged a reputation based on the exceptional quality of its guns. Its side-by-sides remain esteemed for not only their aesthetic signatures – arcaded fences, protruding tumbler pivots, and T-shape safeties – but also for superb balance and handling, as well as the boring of barrels and chokes.

Most Woodwards were built to very best London standards, but there are exceptions – plainer sidelocks are sometimes encountered as well as the occasional boxlock. Many were engraved with a tight scroll pattern with the Woodward name engraved in a parchment motif on the sides of the action.

From 1948 to 1997, the Woodward name was essentially put in cold storage by Purdey, till a booming economy and demand by collectors heralded a comeback. Since 1997, however, new Woodward over/unders and side-by-sides have been available, the former almost identical to the original design and the latter built as conventional Rogers-action guns. Typically they have been engraved with traditional Woodward scroll. Both are built entirely in the Purdey factory to the standards the firm remains famous for.

For more information, *see*
James Purdey & Sons entry.

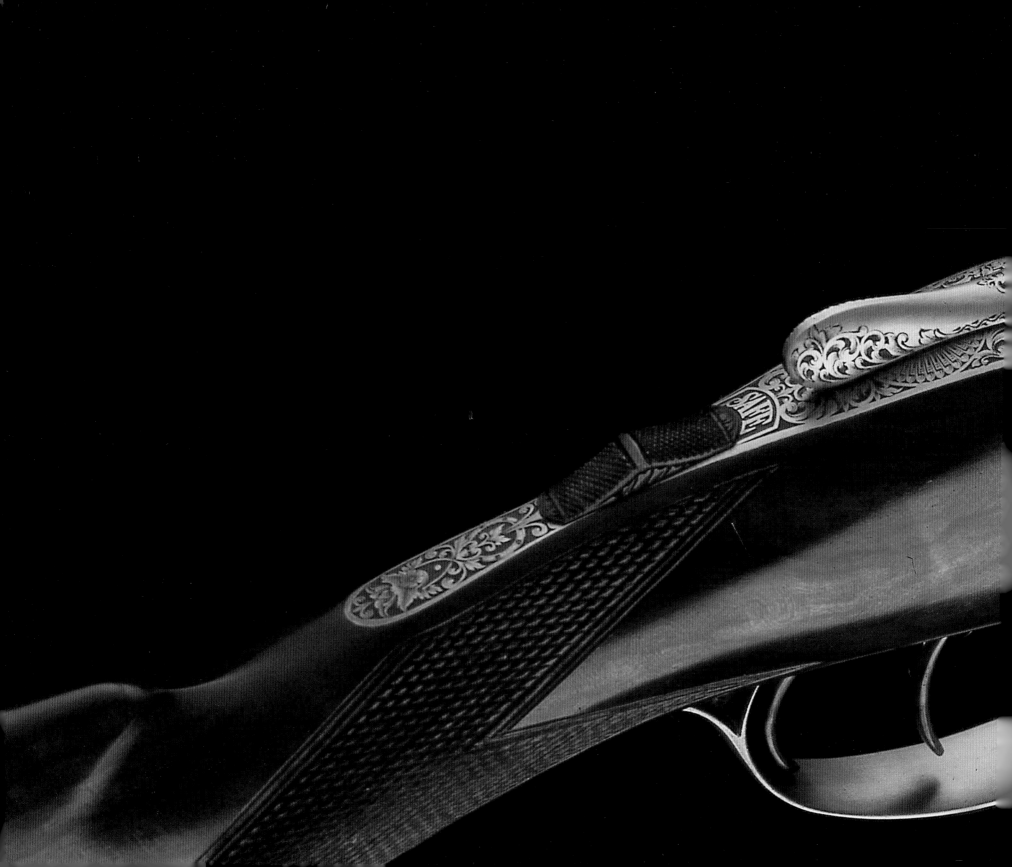